TECHNICAL REPORT

A Cost-Benefit Analysis of the National Guard Youth ChalleNGe Program

Francisco Perez-Arce • Louay Constant • David S. Loughran • Lynn A. Karoly

Sponsored by the National Guard Youth Foundation

The research described in this report was sponsored by the National Guard Youth Foundation and was conducted jointly by RAND Labor and Population and the Forces and Resources Policy Center of the RAND National Defense Research Institute.

Library of Congress Cataloging-in-Publication Data is available for this publication.

ISBN: 978-0-8330-6030-3

Cover photo: courtesy of the National Guard Youth Foundation

Published 2012 by the RAND Corporation
1776 Main Street, P.O. Box 2138, Santa Monica, CA 90407-2138
1200 South Hayes Street, Arlington, VA 22202-5050
4570 Fifth Avenue, Suite 600, Pittsburgh, PA 15213-2665
RAND URL: http://www.rand.org/
To order RAND documents or to obtain additional information, contact
Distribution Services: Telephone: (310) 451-7002;
Fax: (310) 451-6915; Email: order@rand.org

Preface

This technical report presents the results of a cost-benefit analysis of the National Guard Youth ChalleNGe program, an intensive 17-month program intended to alter the life course of 16- to 18-year-old high school dropouts. The cost-benefit analysis is based on the results of a rigorous program evaluation employing random assignment of a sample of applicants eligible for admission to the program between 2005 and 2007. This report will be of interest to state and federal legislatures, foundations, and other organizations that fund the ChalleNGe program and to policymakers more broadly interested in the social returns to intensive, residential programs such as ChalleNGe that target high school dropouts.

The research was sponsored by the National Guard Youth Foundation and was conducted jointly by RAND Labor and Population and the Forces and Resources Policy Center of the RAND National Defense Research Institute (NDRI). NDRI is a federally funded research and development center sponsored by the Office of the Secretary of Defense, the Joint Staff, the Unified Combatant Commands, the Navy, the Marine Corps, the defense agencies, and the defense Intelligence Community.

Comments regarding this report are welcome and may be addressed to the project leader, David Loughran, by email at David_Loughran@rand.org. For more information about the RAND Corporation, RAND Labor and Population, and the Forces and Resources Policy Center, please visit us at www.rand.org.

Contents

Figures

Tables

Summary

According to the most recent data compiled by the National Center for Education Statistics (NCES), about 10 percent of 18- to 24-year-olds in the United States are neither enrolled in high school nor have they received a high school diploma or alternative high school credential such as the General Educational Development (GED) credential; 25 percent of high school freshman fail to graduate from high school within four years. Decades of research show that these high school dropouts are more likely to commit crimes, abuse drugs and alcohol, have children out of wedlock, earn low wages, be un- or underemployed, and suffer poor health than are individuals who successfully complete high school. The ChalleNGe program, an intensive residential and mentoring program for high school dropouts ages 16–18 currently operating in 27 states and Puerto Rico and graduating more than 8,200 young people each year, seeks to avert these negative outcomes.

The research described in this report estimates the social return on investment in the ChalleNGe program through a rigorous quantitative assessment of the monetary costs of operating the program and the benefits it generates by altering the life course of its participants. It concludes that the estimated return on investment in the ChalleNGe program supports ongoing public investment in it. This cost-benefit analysis will be of use to federal and state legislators, private foundations, and other decisionmakers as they consider maintaining and perhaps increasing investment in the ChalleNGe program in an era of increasing fiscal austerity.

Background

ChalleNGe program participants, called cadets, are housed together, often on a National Guard base or at a training center, for the first 22 weeks of the program. During these weeks, the program immerses cadets in a quasi-military environment in which they focus on discipline, academic excellence, teamwork, physical fitness, leadership, and service to the community. The program encourages cadets to obtain a GED and to seek further education and training or employment during the one-year post-residential phase of the program. Individuals ages 16–18 who have dropped out or been expelled from high school and are U.S. citizens or legal residents, un- or underemployed, drug free, physically and mentally capable of participating in the program, and have either no police record or a police record limited to juvenile status offenses are eligible to apply for admission to a ChalleNGe program in their state of residence.

Beginning in 2005, with the support the Department of Defense (DoD) and a variety of nonprofit foundations, MDRC, an independent, nonprofit, nonpartisan social policy research organization, designed and implemented a rigorous evaluation of the ChalleNGe program at ten ChalleNGe sites, employing random assignment. This program evaluation demonstrated strong causal effects of being admitted to the ChalleNGe program on educational attainment and employment. Thirty-six months following randomization, admission to the program had increased GED attainment by 22 percentage points, traditional high school degree attainment by 4 percentage points, some college attendance by 16 percentage points, vocational training and employment by 7 percentage points, and annual earnings by $2,266 (an increase of 20 percent). The evaluation also found some evidence that admission to the ChalleNGe program lowered criminal activity 9 and 21 months after randomization, but these effects were no longer evident 36 months after randomization.

Valuing Costs and Benefits of the ChalleNGe Program

Employing individual site budget data for the ten ChalleNGe sites that participated in the program evaluation, supplemented with information on off-budget costs obtained through interviews with site directors, we estimate that the present discounted value (PDV) of operating costs total $11,633 per ChalleNGe admittee.[1] We estimate additional opportunity costs associated with operating the program—the value of the time spent by ChalleNGe applicants, admittees, and mentors that could have been spent in some other productive activity net of in-kind benefits received by program participants—of $2,058 per admittee.

As noted above, the ChalleNGe program evaluation indicates that its principal benefit is to increase educational attainment, employment, and earnings. Those program effects were observed 36 months following randomization when the ChalleNGe admittees were, on average, only 20 years old. However, research suggests that the benefits of obtaining higher levels of education accrue over an entire lifetime. Thus, to estimate the full benefits of the ChalleNGe program, we must first estimate how education affects lifetime earnings. We estimate this relationship employing data from the 1979 cohort of the National Longitudinal Survey of Youth (NLSY79), a nationally representative longitudinal survey of 12,686 men and women ages 14–22 in 1979.

Consistent with other published research, our empirical estimates indicate substantial effects of receiving a high school diploma and attending a year or more of college on the present discounted value of lifetime earnings but no statistically significant effect of obtaining a GED or participating in vocational training. Applying these empirical estimates to the estimated treatment effects obtained by the ChalleNGe program evaluation yields present discounted value of lifetime earnings benefits (net of the cost of education) totaling $38,654 per admittee.

We employ a similar method to estimate how the increased educational attainment induced by the ChalleNGe program affects social welfare dependency, and we generate separate estimates of the value of the effect of ChalleNGe admission on criminal activity 9 and 21 months following randomization and on service to the community during the residential phase of the program. The present discounted value of estimated benefits generated by the ChalleNGe program for these outcomes totals $1,334 per admittee.

---

[1]   Under our baseline assumptions, all costs and benefits were discounted to the year of admission to the ChalleNGe program at a rate of 3 percent. All dollar figures are expressed in 2010 dollars.

Comparing Costs and Benefits of the ChalleNGe Program

Table S.1 summarizes our estimates of the costs and benefits of the ChalleNGe program assuming that the social discount rate is 3 percent. The discount rate assumes that individuals value current consumption over future consumption; a discount rate of 3 percent is consistent with current rates of interest on long-term treasury bonds and government cost-benefit guidance. The baseline estimates also assume an efficiency loss attributable to taxation (also referred to as "deadweight loss" of taxation) amounting to 15 percent of the change in tax revenue induced by the program. Given these baseline assumptions (which we relax in various sensitivity analyses), the present discounted value of operating and opportunity costs totals $15,436 whereas the present discounted value of social benefits totals $40,985.

Subtracting the estimated present discounted value of costs from benefits, we find that, for each admitted cadet, the program generates net benefits of $25,549. Total benefits of $40,985 are 2.66 times total costs, implying that the ChalleNGe program generates $2.66 in benefits for every dollar spent on the program. The estimated return on investment (net benefits divided by costs) in the ChalleNGe program is 166 percent. Because higher educational attainment yields benefits to individuals and society that are not fully captured in the outcomes con-

Table S.1
Baseline Cost-Benefit Comparison

Item	PDV Benefit per Admittee ($2010)
Costs	
Operating costs	−$11,633
Opportunity costs	−$2,058
Deadweight loss of taxation (15%)	−$1,745
Total costs	−$15,436
Benefits	
Lifetime earnings	$43,514
Cost of education	−$4,860
Social welfare dependency	$249
Criminal activity	$662
Service to the community	$423
Deadweight loss of taxation (15%)	$997
Total benefits	$40,985
Cost-benefit comparison	
Net benefits	$25,549
Benefit-cost ratio	2.66
Return on investment	166%
Internal rate of return	6.4%

NOTE: Estimates assume a social discount rate of 3 percent.

sidered here, it is likely that, all else equal, these benefit estimates understate the social return on investment in the ChalleNGe program, although to what extent is not known.

However, it is important to acknowledge that the "baseline" benefit-cost ratio of 2.66 is sensitive to the approach taken to forecasting future earnings of ChalleNGe admittees and the assumed social discount rate. Table S.2 presents estimated benefit-cost ratios in which we compute estimated earnings benefits employing six different empirical models (by which we mean empirically estimated statistical relationships between earnings and education), for three different social discount rates, assuming a deadweight loss factor of 15 percent. The six different earnings models are as follows:

- **Baseline model.**
- **Complete less than one year of college model.** This model assumes that the effect of ChalleNGe admission is to increase the probability of attending one year of college by age 20 but not the probability of completing that year of college.
- **No postsecondary degree models.** These two models assume that the effect of ChalleNGe admission is to increase the probability of attending one year of college by age 20 but not to increase the probability of (1) obtaining an advanced or professional degree such as a master's or law degree or (2) more restrictively, a four-year college degree.
- **NLSY97 model.** This model employs data from the NLSY97, a nationally representative cohort of American youth ages 12–18 in 1997. This model has the advantage of estimating the effect of education on earnings in a birth cohort that is closer in age to the ChalleNGe program evaluation sample but has the disadvantage of observing their labor market earnings only through ages 24–29 (the last available survey wave is 2009).
- **Causal effect of education model.** Estimating the effect of education on earnings is complicated by the fact that we cannot observe all of the factors that affect both educational attainment and earnings. This model employs parameter estimates reported in published studies that employ "natural experiments" to isolate the causal effect of education on earnings.

At a social discount rate of 3 percent, the most conservative estimate of the benefit-cost ratio is 1.54, which assumes that ChalleNGe admission has no effect on the probability of obtaining a four-year college degree. On the other hand, employing widely cited returns to

Table S.2
Benefit-Cost Ratio, by Lifetime Earnings Model and Social Discount Rate

Earnings Model	Social Discount Rate		
	3%	5%	7%
Baseline	2.66	1.46	0.82
Complete less than one year of college	1.78	1.11	0.74
No advanced or professional degree	2.42	1.32	0.73
No four-year college degree	1.54	0.85	0.47
NLSY97	3.17	2.03	1.38
Causal effect of education	2.71–4.98	1.62–3.13	1.05–2.08

NOTE: Estimates assume a deadweight loss factor of 15 percent.

educational attainment published in the economics literature or data from the more recent 1997 NLSY cohort yields benefit-cost ratios of 2.71–4.98 and 3.17, respectively.

Because the earnings benefits attributable to higher education occur in the future, whereas the costs of the ChalleNGe program occur in the present, the benefit-cost ratio declines rapidly with the social discount rate. At social discount rates above 6.4 percent (the "internal rate of return"), the ChalleNGe program no longer yields positive social returns under the assumptions of the baseline model. The benefit-cost ratio, though, is not nearly as sensitive to the choice of deadweight loss factor, since the deadweight loss of taxation increases both costs and benefits.

Policy Implications

Under baseline assumptions, these cost-benefit comparisons suggest that continued operation of existing ChalleNGe sites will yield substantial net benefits, albeit largely in the form of private benefits to program participants from higher earnings rather than benefits to the public sector and other members of society. This analytical conclusion supports continued public investment in the ChalleNGe program, especially considering that educational attainment likely yields benefits to individuals and society that are not fully captured in the outcomes considered here and that the estimated return on investment in the ChalleNGe program is considerably higher than that estimated for other rigorously evaluated social programs, such as Job Corps, Big Brothers Big Sisters, and state welfare-to-work programs that seek to alter the life course of disadvantaged youth and young adults.

The extent to which these cost-benefit estimates lend support to proposals to expand the ChalleNGe program to serve more youth depends on several additional factors. First, program effects achieved at the ChalleNGe evaluation sites must be generalizable to future applicant cohorts. This is perhaps reasonable to assume, provided that the program continues to serve what appears to be a relatively advantaged population of high school dropouts. Second, one must assume that the average cost of serving a larger population of dropouts does not increase significantly relative to the estimated benefits. Again, this may be reasonable to assume, provided that the program expansion targets a similarly situated population of dropouts.

Acknowledgments

This cost-benefit analysis benefited enormously from the rigorous program evaluation conducted by MDRC. We are indebted to Dan Bloom and Megan Millenky of MDRC for helping us to understand the program evaluation, providing us with unpublished tabulations from the evaluation, and reviewing an earlier draft of this report. We also wish to thank John Permaul and Chad Vogelsang of the National Guard Bureau for providing us with access to detailed budget information for the ten ChalleNGe evaluation sites, helping us to understand those budgets, and facilitating interviews with ChalleNGe site directors. This research also benefited from the input and guidance provided by the director of the National Guard Youth Foundation (NGYF), Jim Tinkham, and NGYF board members Gail Dady, Christopher Jehn, and Kim Wincup. Finally, we thank our RAND colleagues Paul Heaton, Emmett Keeler, and John Winkler for conducting detailed reviews of this report and providing us with constructive criticism throughout the research process.

Abbreviations

ACS	American Community Survey
AFQT	Armed Forces Qualification Test
ASVAB	Armed Services Vocational Aptitude Battery
CPI	consumer price index
CPS	Current Population Survey
DoD	Department of Defense
DRMO	Defense Reutilization and Marketing Office
GAO	Government Accountability Office
GED	General Educational Development (credential)
NCES	National Center for Education Statistics
NDRI	National Defense Research Institute
NGB	National Guard Bureau
NGYF	National Guard Youth Foundation
NLSY	National Longitudinal Survey of Youth
OMB	Office of Management and Budget
PDV	present discounted value
PDVE	present discounted value of lifetime earnings
USDA	U.S. Department of Agriculture

CHAPTER ONE

Introduction

According to the most recent data compiled by the National Center for Education Statistics (NCES), about 10 percent of 18- to 24-year-olds in the United States are neither enrolled in high school nor have received a high school diploma or alternative high school credential such as the General Educational Development (GED) credential; 25 percent of high school freshman fail to graduate from high school within four years (Chapman et al., 2011).[1] Decades of research show that these high school dropouts are more likely to commit crimes, abuse drugs and alcohol, have children out of wedlock, earn low wages, be un- or underemployed, and suffer poor health than are individuals who successfully complete high school.[2] The National Guard Youth ChalleNGe program, an intensive residential and mentoring program for high school dropouts ages 16–18, seeks to avert these negative outcomes.

The research summarized in this report estimates the social return on investment in the ChalleNGe program through a rigorous quantitative assessment of the monetary costs of operating the program and the benefits it generates by altering the life course of its participants. This cost-benefit analysis will be of use to federal and state legislators, private foundations, and other decisionmakers as they consider maintaining and perhaps increasing investment in the ChalleNGe program in an era of increasing fiscal austerity.

ChalleNGe program participants, called cadets, are housed together, often on a National Guard base or training center, for the first 22 weeks of the program. During these weeks, the program immerses cadets in a quasi-military environment in which they focus on discipline, academic excellence, teamwork, physical fitness, leadership, and service to the community. A major objective of the ChalleNGe program is to prepare cadets for the GED exam, which is given at the end of the residential phase of the program. The program then encourages cadets to seek further education and training or civilian or military employment during the one-year post-residential phase of the program. Structured mentoring during the post-residential phase is intended to help cadets maintain and build upon the skills they have developed and work toward meeting the goals of the "Life Plan" they outlined during the residential phase of the program.[3]

---

[1] Some (e.g., Heckman and LaFontaine, 2010) argue that the NCES approach to calculating the dropout rate substantially underestimates the true rate due to limitations of the Current Population Survey (CPS), which is the source of data for the NCES statistics. The freshman graduation rate is the number of diplomas awarded in a given year divided by the average number of 8th, 9th, and 10th grade students two, three, and four years earlier.

[2] See, for example, McCaul et al. (1992); Lochner and Moretti (2004); Oreopoulos (2007); and Black, Devereux, and Salvanes (2008).

[3] Bloom, Gardenhire-Crooks, and Mandsager (2009) provide a detailed description of the ChalleNGe program. Readers might also refer to the ChalleNGe program website.

There are 34 ChalleNGe program sites currently operating in 27 states and Puerto Rico. Most ChalleNGe programs serve between 200 and 400 cadets per year. Between its inception in 1993 and 2010, the ChalleNGe program in total enrolled 127,744 applicants and graduated 96,122 cadets (National Guard Bureau [NGB], 2011). These 34 programs are administered by the NGB, under the auspices of the Assistant Secretary of Defense, Reserve Affairs, through cooperative agreements with participating state governments. The federal government funds 75 percent of program costs; state governments fund the remaining 25 percent of program costs.

Youth between the ages of 16 and 18 who have dropped out or been expelled from a secondary school and are U.S. citizens or legal residents, un- or underemployed, drug-free, physically and mentally capable of participating in the program, and have either no police record or a police record limited to juvenile status offenses are eligible to apply for admission to a ChalleNGe program in their state of residence.[4] The program is open to both males and females, but about 80 percent of cadets are male (Bloom, Gardenhire-Crooks, and Mandsager, 2009). Individuals might be encouraged to apply by their parents, school principal or guidance counselor, juvenile justice personnel, youth organizations, or other professionals who might otherwise serve high school dropouts. Most ChalleNGe programs employ recruiters who market the program in their state, often by making formal presentations at schools, community centers, and the like. Some ChalleNGe programs also advertise in local media (Bloom, Gardenhire-Crooks, and Mandsager, 2009).

For a variety of reasons, it is clear that individuals who participate in the ChalleNGe program do not represent a random sample of the universe of high school dropouts. First, as just noted, cadets must meet certain eligibility criteria. Second, ChalleNGe programs have discretion over how to target their recruitment efforts. Bloom, Gardenhire-Crooks, and Mandsager (2009), for example, note that some programs do not target inner-city youth, whereas other programs target recruitment to achieve a particular racial balance or select cadets they think are likely to succeed in the program. Finally, setting aside eligibility criteria and targeted recruitment efforts, participation in a ChalleNGe program is voluntary. Thus, individuals choose to apply and, if admitted, enroll in ChalleNGe, and that choice is likely to be a function of important characteristics of these individuals, such as motivation and discipline, that set them apart from the overall population of high school dropouts.

The voluntary nature of the ChalleNGe program makes it difficult to evaluate whether the program is successful in changing the life course of its participants, since the factors driving individuals to participate, many of which cannot be observed empirically, may be correlated with the outcomes of interest. In 2005, however, with the support the Department of Defense and a variety of nonprofit foundations, MDRC, an independent nonprofit, nonpartisan social policy research organization, designed and implemented a rigorous evaluation of the ChalleNGe program (hereafter referred to as the "ChalleNGe program evaluation"), employing random assignment that yields estimates of the causal effect of the program on a variety of important life outcomes. As explained in detail in the next chapter, the ChalleNGe program evaluation randomly assigned a sample of eligible applicants to be either admitted or denied admission to the program. The evaluation then measured educational, labor market, criminal

---

[4]   Cadets must enter the program before their 19th birthday. With respect to criminal activity, applicants must be not currently on parole or probation for anything other than juvenile status offenses; not serving time or awaiting sentencing; and not under indictment, accused, or convicted of a felony offense (per DoD guidance, DODI 1025.8, 2002).

justice, health, and other outcomes of admitted and nonadmitted applicants approximately 9, 21, and 36 months following entry into the study.

The ChalleNGe program evaluation found significant effects of being randomized into the admitted group[5] on educational attainment and employment at all three points in time. The evaluation also found some evidence that admission to the ChalleNGe program lowered criminal activity and improved self-reported health, but these effects were no longer evident at the time of the 36-month survey.

The present study monetizes the social benefits of the ChalleNGe program as measured by the ChalleNGe program evaluation and compares them to the social costs of operating the program. The benefits of the ChalleNGe program accrue largely from increased labor market earnings attributable to increases in educational attainment, and the costs accrue largely from the program's operating expenses. However, our estimates account for the full range of social costs and benefits attributable to the program. Although the credibility of this cost-benefit study is greatly enhanced by the availability of the results of a random assignment program evaluation, we must acknowledge that there remains considerable uncertainty in the reported cost-benefit estimate due to uncertainty in estimating the effect of education on lifetime earnings and other outcomes, uncertainty in other key parameters such as the social discount rate and the deadweight loss of taxation, and sampling error inherent in the estimated program effects.[6] Consequently, in summarizing the results of this cost-benefit analysis, we report both "baseline" cost-benefit estimates and a much wider range of estimates employing alternative assumptions.

The remainder of this report has the following structure. Chapter Two summarizes the results of the ChalleNGe program evaluation, presents an overview of our cost-benefit methodology, and discusses a number of important limitations with our approach, many of which are inherent in cost-benefit analysis. Chapters Three and Four provide further details on how we evaluate program costs and benefits and reports those estimates. Chapter Five then compares estimated costs and benefits employing a number of standard metrics (e.g., net benefit, cost-benefit ratio, return on investment, internal rate of return), presents the results of a variety of sensitivity analyses, and shows how costs and benefits are allocated across ChalleNGe admittees, the public sector, and the rest of private society. Chapter Six concludes.

---

[5] As we explain in the next chapter, those in the admitted group did not all enroll in or graduate from the ChalleNGe program.

[6] This research did not have access to the program evaluation micro-data, and so it was not possible to compute standard errors for the benefit estimates without making strong assumptions about the correlation of the standard errors associated with the various estimated treatment effects. Moreover, such a computation would require making assumptions about the correlation of the error terms between the estimated treatment effects and their estimated effects on earnings in ancillary data.

CHAPTER TWO

Methodology

This cost-benefit analysis benefits from the rigorous evaluation of the ChalleNGe program conducted by MDRC, the results of which were reported in three documents published between 2009 and 2011 (Bloom, Gardenhire-Crooks, and Mandsager, 2009; Millenky, Bloom, and Dillon, 2010; Millenky et al., 2011). The first section of this chapter describes the ChalleNGe program evaluation and its key results and explains how those results can be interpreted. A subsequent section then explains the general features of our cost-benefit analysis in terms of the types of costs and benefits evaluated and how we account for discounting and deadweight loss.

The ChalleNGe Program Evaluation

The ChalleNGe program evaluation employed random assignment to overcome the formidable problem of selection bias attributable to unobserved heterogeneity in the population of youth who do and do not participate in ChalleNGe. Randomization occurred among the population of applicants to a set of 18 ChalleNGe class cycles across ten ChalleNGe programs located in ten different states. Sixteen of the 18 class cycles occurred in 2006; there was one class cycle each in 2005 and 2007 (see Table 2.1). MDRC excluded from the evaluation eligible applicants who would have been under age 17 on the last day of the residential phase of the class cycle for which they applied.[1]

MDRC required that participating programs demonstrate both stable staffing and oversubscription. Oversubscription means that the programs selected for the evaluation typically received more eligible applicants than they could serve, which ensured that the evaluation would not have the effect of reducing the number of individuals admitted to and ultimately served by the program. Twelve programs in operation in 2005 (about half the programs in operation at that time) met these criteria and agreed to participate in the evaluation.

The ChalleNGe program evaluation was originally designed to include two class cycles per program and to obtain a sample size of 2,500 youths. However, in the end, not all 12 programs succeeded in attracting enough eligible applicants to achieve the desired level of oversubscription (at least 25 more eligible applicants than the program could serve). Two programs, Arizona and Virginia, could not achieve a sufficient level of oversubscription in any of the class cycles, and three programs (California, New Mexico, and Wisconsin) achieved oversubscription in only one class cycle. Six programs—Florida, Georgia, Illinois, North Carolina,

---

[1] In some class cycles, women were also excluded from the evaluation because the number of female applicants was too small to facilitate randomization without reducing the number of women served below acceptable levels (personal communication with Dan Bloom, MDRC, October 26, 2011).

Table 2.1
ChalleNGe Class Cycles Participating in the ChalleNGe Program Evaluation

State	Site	First Year of Operation	2005	2006		2007
			Cycle 2	Cycle 1	Cycle 2	Cycle 1
California	Camp San Luis Obispo	1998			X	
Florida	Camp Blanding	2001		X	X	
Georgia	Fort Gordon	2000		X	X	
Illinois	Rantoul	1993		X	X	
Michigan	Battle Creek	1999	X	X	X	
Mississippi	Camp Shelby	1994			X	X
New Mexico	Roswell	2001			X	
North Carolina	Salemsburg	1994		X	X	
Texas	Galveston	1999		X	X	
Wisconsin	Fort McCoy	1998			X	

SOURCE: Bloom, Gardenhire-Crooks, and Mandsager (2009).

Mississippi, and Texas—achieved oversubscription in two class cycles and one program—Michigan—achieved oversubscription in three class cycles.

The participating states all agreed to use random assignment to select eligible applicants for acceptance into the ChalleNGe program. Eligible applicants who were not selected for acceptance were not allowed to reapply for later class cycles. Across all 18 class cycles, 3,074 eligible applicants took part in the evaluation; 2,320 were randomly accepted into the program (the treatment group) and 754 were randomly denied admission (the control group).

Interpretation of Treatment Effects

The ChalleNGe program evaluation permits analysis of the effect of being accepted for admission to the ChalleNGe program among a population that met the program's eligibility criteria. A significant number of applicants accepted for admission during the evaluation (which we will refer to as "admittees") did not register, enroll, or ultimately graduate from the residential phase of the program. About 83 percent of the admittees registered for ChalleNGe, 68 percent completed the two-week "Pre-ChalleNGe" assessment and orientation phase of the program, and 53 percent completed the full 22-week residential phase of the program (Bloom, Gardenhire-Crooks, and Mandsager, 2009). These percentages are consistent with registration, enrollment, and graduation rates observed in the overall population of ChalleNGe applicants accepted for admission in all class cycles between 2005 and 2007 (Bloom, Gardenhire-Crooks, and Mandsager, 2009).

Thus, only slightly more than one-half of admittees graduated from the ChalleNGe program, and an even smaller percentage actively participated in the one-year post-residential phase of the program (Bloom, Gardenhire-Crooks, and Mandsager, 2009). This means that the estimated effects of being admitted to the ChalleNGe program, which we will refer to as "treatment effects," do not necessarily correspond to the effects of participating in or graduating from the program. In the program evaluation literature, this type of design is known as "intent-to-treat;" the intention of admitting an individual to the program is to treat them, but there is no guarantee that treatment will occur. We naturally presume that the effect of being admitted to the program will be less than the effect of being served by the program, but that assumption cannot be validated within the ChalleNGe program evaluation study design.

It is also important to acknowledge that the effect of admitting an eligible applicant to the ChalleNGe program will not necessarily be equivalent to the effect of admitting a randomly selected high school dropout to the program. For example, Panel A of Table 2.2 shows that, conditional on age, gender, and race/ethnicity, the average high school dropout is at once less likely to have completed more than 8th grade and more likely to have completed 11th and 12th grades than is the average eligible ChalleNGe applicant. As discussed in Chapter One, it is also likely that even conditional on these observable differences, eligible ChalleNGe applicants differ from the average high school dropout in other important ways, such as their general aptitude, level of motivation, discipline, or respect for authority. The potential influence of

Table 2.2
Selected Characteristics of Eligible ChalleNGe Applicants and the General Population of High School Dropouts

	ChalleNGe Evaluation Sample[a]	2005 ACS[b]	NLSY97[c]
A. Highest grade completed at time of randomization[d]			
8th grade or lower	0.142	0.221	
9th grade	0.314	0.238	
10th grade	0.382	0.293	
11th grade	0.156	0.195	
12th grade	0.006	0.053	
B. Educational attainment three years following randomization[d]			
GED	0.345		0.217
High school diploma	0.266		0.113
Some college	0.188		0.038

NOTE: ACS and NLSY97 estimates are weighted to match the age, gender, and race/ethnicity distribution of the ChalleNGe evaluation sample.

[a] ChalleNGe evaluation sample means at the time of the baseline survey of the full evaluation sample as reported in Bloom, Gardenhire-Crooks, and Mandsager (2009).

[b] Authors' calculation from the 2005 American Community Survey (ACS). The ACS sample is restricted to individuals who are not currently attending school and have not earned a high school diploma or received a GED.

[c] Authors' calculation from the 1997 cohort of the National Longitudinal Survey of Youth (NLSY97). The NSLY97 sample is restricted to individuals ages 16–18 in 2000 who are not currently attending school and have not earned a high school diploma or received a GED. Educational attainment is measured when NLSY97 respondents are ages 19–21.

[d] ChalleNGe control group means at the time of the 36-month survey as reported in Millenky et al. (2011).

these unobservable characteristics is evident in Panel B of Table 2.2, which shows that eligible ChalleNGe applicants who were denied admission (the control group) are considerably more likely to obtain a GED, a high school diploma, and attend some college by ages 19–21 than is the average dropout.

Thus, it is not known whether the average high school dropout would be more or less affected by being admitted to the ChalleNGe program than those individuals who were interested in and eligible to participate. The ChalleNGe program evaluation, which was constrained by its voluntary nature, permits us to draw inferences only about the effect of being admitted to the ChalleNGe program conditional on applying for and being eligible for admission to the program.[2]

Estimated Treatment Effects

The ChalleNGe program surveyed a sample of the treatment and control groups approximately 9, 21, and 36 months following entry into the study (i.e., the date of randomization into the treatment and control groups). The sample for the 9-month survey consisted of 1,018 admittees drawn from the first random assignment cohort for each site (except Michigan, where the first two cohorts were included in the 9-month survey) (Bloom, Gardenhire-Crooks, and Mandsager, 2009). The 21- and 36-month survey samples targeted the same 1,507 admittees. The evaluation sampled admittees at differing rates across sites and random assignment status to minimize the variance of estimated effects when sites are weighted equally in the analysis. The ChalleNGe program evaluation achieved 79 and 78 percent response rates for the 21- and 36-month surveys, respectively; 88 percent of the 36-month survey respondents were also surveyed at 21 months (Millenky, Bloom, and Dillon, 2010; Millenky et al., 2011).

The surveys covered a range of standard demographic, educational, labor market, crime, and health-related outcomes. The causal effect of being admitted to the ChalleNGe program was then estimated by comparing the mean outcomes of the treatment and control groups at different points in time. Although analyses of observable baseline characteristics did not reveal any systematic differences between treatment and control groups due to the randomization process or survey nonresponse, MDRC nonetheless estimated differences in means controlling for a range of baseline characteristics to increase the precision of the resulting treatment effects.[3] The analyses also employed weights so that each of the ten sites contributed equally to the estimated treatment effects regardless of their relative size.

Tables 2.3–2.5 report estimated treatment effects for educational and vocational training outcomes, employment outcomes, criminal activity, and health outcomes. Perhaps the most consistent and pronounced effect of being admitted to the ChalleNGe program is on the receipt of a GED (see Table 2.3). At the time of the 36-month survey, the treatment group was 22 percentage points more likely to have obtained a GED than was the control group.

---

[2] We also note that we must assume estimated treatment effects in the ten oversubscribed program evaluation sites generalize to other ChalleNGe sites.

[3] Millenky et al. (2011) report that, at the time of randomization, the treatment and control groups were generally statistically indistinguishable in terms of age, gender, race/ethnicity, family structure, educational attainment, grades, and health. Small differences in the number of arrests, convictions, public assistance, and drug and alcohol use were observed, but these differences do not point to either the treatment or control groups being systematically more disadvantaged at the time of randomization. Estimated treatment effects control for differences in age, gender, race, whether the sample member was interested in ChalleNGe because he or she wanted to join the military, whether he or she lived in a two-parent household, and highest grade completed.

However, the treatment group was only 3.7 percentage points more likely to have obtained a traditional high school diploma at that juncture, and that difference is not statistically significant at conventional levels. The program evaluation also indicates that the treatment group was considerably more likely to have participated in vocational training (an estimated treatment effect of 0.070) and obtained some college credit (an estimated treatment effect of 0.161). The estimated treatment effects also indicate that the treatment group was 3.6 percentage points more likely to be currently attending college at the time of the 36-month survey. The evaluation sample was on average about 20 years old at this juncture, and so it is not surprising that the estimated effect of being admitted to the ChalleNGe program on receiving a college degree or vocational license or certificate was small and imprecisely estimated.

The ChalleNGe program evaluation also revealed robust effects of being admitted to the ChalleNGe program on employment and earnings (see Table 2.4). At the time of the

Table 2.3
Estimated Treatment Effects of Being Admitted to the ChalleNGe Program: Educational and Vocational Training Outcomes

	Survey Wave		
Outcome	9 Months	21 Months	36 Months
Ever			
High school diploma	0.120***	0.057**	0.037
GED	0.234***	0.265***	0.224***
College credit		0.151***	0.161***
College degree		0.003	0.008*
Vocational training		0.068**	0.070**
License/certificate		0.033	0.019
Currently			
High school	−0.192***	−0.066***	
GED preparation	−0.061**	−0.039**	
High school or GED preparation			-0.019
College courses	0.082***	0.046***	0.036**
Job training	0.039*	0.007	0.016
Last 9–12 months			
High school	−0.182***		
GED preparation	0.150***		
College courses	0.149***		
Vocational training	0.097***		

SOURCES: Bloom, Gardenhire-Crooks, and Mandsager (2009); Millenky, Bloom, and Dillon (2010); Millenky et al. (2011).
*Denotes statistical significance at the 10 percent level.
**Denotes statistical significance at the 5 percent level.
***Denotes statistical significance at the 1 percent level.

36-month survey, the treatment group was 7.1 percentage points more likely to be currently working and 3.9 percentage points more likely to have been employed in the last 12 months (although this latter difference is statistically significant at only the 10 percent level). At the 36-month interval, the estimates indicate that the treatment group had been employed an average of one month more than the control group over the previous 12 months and that they had earned an average of $2,266 more over this same period.

The estimated effect of being admitted to the ChalleNGe program on criminal activity and health is less robust (see Table 2.5). At the time of the 9-month survey, the treatment group was less likely to have been arrested or convicted of a crime and less likely to have been incarcerated than the control group over the previous 9–12 months. At the time of the 21-month survey, the treatment group was still less likely to have been convicted of a crime than the control group but no more likely to have been arrested or charged with a crime. The treatment group also on average reported being involved in fewer violent incidents and committing fewer property crimes. None of these treatment effects, though, were evident at the time of the 36-month survey.

In terms of health, the treatment group was more likely to report being in very good or excellent health and less likely to be obese at the time of the 9-month survey. These positive

Table 2.4
Estimated Treatment Effects of Being Admitted to the ChalleNGe Program: Labor Market Outcomes

	Survey Wave		
Outcome	9 Months	21 Months	36 Months
Currently			
Enlisted		0.047***	0.011
Working	0.091***	0.049*	0.071**
Working full-time	0.096***	0.049*	0.029
Weekly earnings		$39***	$30*
Last 9–12 months			
Worked	0.028		
Last 12 months			
Employed			0.039*
Earnings			$2,266***
Months employed			0.900***
Ever			
Enlisted			0.011

SOURCES: Bloom, Gardenhire-Crooks, and Mandsager (2009); Millenky, Bloom, and Dillon (2010); Millenky et al. (2011).

* Denotes statistical significance at the 10 percent level.

** Denotes statistical significance at the 5 percent level.

*** Denotes statistical significance at the 1 percent level.

Table 2.5
Estimated Treatment Effects of Being Admitted to the ChalleNGe Program:
Criminal Activity and Health Outcomes

Outcome	Survey Wave		
	9 Months	21 Months	36 Months
Criminal Activity			
Last 9–12 months			
Arrested	–0.058**		
Convicted	–0.044**		
Incarcerated	–0.082**		
Last 12 months			
Arrested		0.009	–0.008
Charged		0.003	0.036
Convicted		–0.042**	0.028
Violent incidents		–0.033	0.042
No. violent incidents		–0.400**	0.100
Property incidents		–0.079***	-0.023
No. property incidents		–0.400***	-0.100
Health			
Currently			
Very good/excellent health	0.084***	0.016	0.040
Overweight	0.042	0.010	0.061**
Obese	–0.043**	–0.015	–0.007

SOURCES: Bloom, Gardenhire-Crooks, and Mandsager (2009); Millenky, Bloom, and Dillon (2010); Millenky et al. (2011).

* Denotes statistical significance at the 10 percent level.

** Denotes statistical significance at the 5 percent level.

*** Denotes statistical significance at the 1 percent level.

health effects are not evident at the time of the 21- and 36-month surveys. Indeed, the treatment group is 6.1 percentage points more likely to be overweight at the time of the 36-month survey. The ChalleNGe program evaluation also shows that the treatment group was 5 percentage points more likely to have ever used illegal drugs, 8 percentage points less likely to always use birth control, and 3.5 percentage points more likely to have had a child than the control group at the time of the 36-month survey, although this later treatment effect is not statistically significant and none of these treatment effects were statistically significant at the time of the 21-month survey (Millenky, Bloom, and Dillon, 2010; Millenky et al., 2011). The evaluation revealed no consistent and statistically significant effects of being admitted to the ChalleNGe program on various life skills and civic engagement (Millenky et al., 2011).

General Features of the Cost-Benefit Analysis

As we explain in detail in Chapter Four, our baseline approach to valuing program benefits focuses on valuing the estimated effect of ChalleNGe admission on educational attainment and vocational training. The most obvious effect of educational attainment and vocational training is on labor market outcomes such as employment and earnings (see, for example Card, 1999). Educational attainment is correlated with many other outcomes that have private and social value, including less social welfare dependency, lower criminal activity, better health, greater stated happiness, greater civic engagement, and improved economic growth (Oreopoulos and Salvanes, 2011; Lochner, 2011; Moretti, 2004). The causal relationship between educational attainment and these other "nonpecuniary" outcomes, however, is much less well established, and so we focus this cost-benefit analysis on labor market outcomes, principally lifetime earnings, though we do estimate the effect of educational attainment on social welfare dependency and value the observed effects of ChalleNGe admission on crime at the time of the 9- and 21-month surveys.[4] Thus, this cost-benefit analysis might understate benefits to the extent that the increase in educational attainment caused by ChalleNGe admission yields these other nonpecuniary returns.

In the chapters to follow, we present a range of cost-benefit estimates employing different methods for forecasting earnings and other pecuniary effects attributable to ChalleNGe admission and a range of assumptions for such key parameters as the social discount rate and deadweight loss factor, but a set of assumptions, which we detail here, is common to all reported estimates. First, we estimate costs and benefits per ChalleNGe admittee, since the ChalleNGe program evaluation design yields estimated treatment effects that can be interpreted only as the effect of being admitted to the ChalleNGe program. And since the ChalleNGe program evaluation employed weights such that each of the ten ChalleNGe sites contributes equally to the estimated treatment effects, the estimated costs per admittee are first computed for each ChalleNGe site and then averaged across the ten sites to arrive at a cost per admittee that also weights all ten sites equally.

Second, we present costs and benefits in terms of their present discounted value (PDV) at age 17, which corresponds to the modal age of admittees during the residential phase of the ChalleNGe program. Discounting assumes that people, individually and collectively, from the perspective of today, value future consumption less than current consumption, which is a key assumption of economic theory. Most ChalleNGe costs are not discounted, since they mostly occur during the residential phase of the program, but the benefits of the program are discounted considerably, since they largely occur after the residential phase. Labor market earnings effects, for example, are estimated at every age between ages 19 and 65.

There is no agreed upon discount rate for use in cost-benefit analyses. The U.S. Government Accountability Office (GAO) recommends using a discount rate consistent with the federal government's long-term cost of borrowing (the interest rate on 30-year treasury bonds is currently about 3 percent), whereas the Office of Management and Budget (OMB) recommends using a discount rate that corresponds to the pretax return on private-sector invest-

---

[4]   We also monetize the service-to-community component of ChalleNGe. We do not monetize the weight, contraception, and drug use treatment effects estimated at the time of the 36-month survey. Those treatment effects were not evident at the time of the 21-month survey, making it less certain that they will persist in the future. One could monetize these treatment effects for a single year (as we do with criminal activity), but those dollar amounts are likely to be inconsequential.

ments (which was about 7 percent at the time the recommendation was made in 1992) (GAO, 1991; OMB, 1992). Our baseline estimates assume a social discount rate of 3 percent, which is consistent with most cost-benefit analyses of programs targeting children and young adults (Karoly, 2008). Sensitivity analyses show how the cost-benefit estimates vary with alternative discount rates and compute the discount rate at which the present discounted value of benefits just equals the present discounted value of costs (otherwise known as the internal rate of return). We employ the consumer price index to express all costs and benefits in 2010 dollars.

Finally, we account for the fact that raising funds necessary to pay for ChalleNGe through taxation is expected to yield deadweight loss—the efficiency loss implicit in driving a wedge between the true cost of an economic good and the price actually paid. However, the net effect of ChalleNGe on deadweight loss depends on whether ChalleNGe admission, on net, increases or decreases tax revenue. On the one hand, tax revenue must increase to pay for ChalleNGe but, on the other hand, higher earnings and decreased social welfare and criminal justice expenditures attributable to ChalleNGe admission offset the need to raise this tax revenue. We estimate deadweight loss by first computing the net change in the tax burden (assuming that labor market earnings in this population are taxed at an average rate of 20 percent) caused by the ChalleNGe program and by then applying a range of deadweight loss factors to that total. There is no consensus on what this deadweight loss factor should be; our baseline estimates follow Barnett, Belfield, and Nores (2005) in assuming a deadweight loss factor of 15 percent. Sensitivity analyses show the effect of assuming deadweight loss factors between 0 and 100 percent. For expositional reasons, we apply the deadweight loss factors in Chapter Five when comparing costs and benefits but not in Chapters Three and Four, in which we describe our approach to valuing program costs and benefits.

CHAPTER THREE

Valuing Program Costs

We estimate the total social cost per individual admitted to the ChalleNGe program during the evaluation period to be $13,691. Total social cost encompasses both operating costs and opportunity costs. *Operating costs* include the site-specific expenditures made by each of the ten sites in each of the evaluated class cycles and a share of the operating costs incurred at the national level by the National Guard Bureau. *Opportunity costs* refer to the value of time spent by ChalleNGe applicants, cadets, and their families applying to and participating in the ChalleNGe program as well as the time volunteered by mentors during the post-residential phase of the program. The following sections explain our approach to estimating these two components of total costs and report the results of that estimation.

Operating Costs

The costs associated with operating the ten ChalleNGe sites during the residential and post-residential phases of the relevant class cycles were compiled using site-level budgets for 2005, 2006, and 2007.[1] Each program site is required to submit an annual budget, typically covering two class cycles, using the ChalleNGe Budget Management and Reporting System. In cases in which only one class cycle in a given year participated in the ChalleNGe program evaluation, we allocated costs to the evaluated class cycle in proportion to the number of admittees in that cycle.

Broad categories of costs reported in the site-level budgets include

- salaries and benefits of full-time, part-time, and some contract staff, and stipends paid to cadets
- facilities lease, maintenance, and utilities
- indoor and outdoor furnishings
- transportation and travel of cadets and staff
- dining operations
- educational, administrative, and other facilities-related supplies and equipment
- apparel for cadets
- educational, medical, and other contracted services
- telecommunications and computing hardware, maintenance, and use
- outreach and security services including marketing and recruiting expenses.

---

[1] Interviews with site directors confirmed that budgets were fully expended.

Not all sites reported costs associated with each of these items. For example, each site reported costs associated with staff salaries and benefits, but not all sites reported allowances for cadets. At some sites, educational services were provided by members of the full-time staff, whereas in others, instructional services were contracted out through the local school district. Moreover, some sites reported costs associated with rent or lease of facilities, whereas other sites had existing agreements with local or state entities to use facilities at little to no direct cost to the program.

We conducted interviews with the directors of the ten program sites that participated in the ChalleNGe program evaluation to clarify certain aspects of the budgets and to identify additional costs that might not have been included. For example, only four of the ten sites accounted for the cost of renting or leasing the facilities needed to run the program in their budgets in all relevant class cycles. Two of the sites with missing rental value data in their budgets provided this information to us during interviews. For the remaining four sites with missing rental value data in their budgets, we estimated this value using data on average price per square foot for five of the sites that did report this information—$2.64 (2005), $2.72 (2006), and $2.86 (2007)—and estimates of the square footage of facilities obtained from these same interviews.[2]

Additional cost items not included in most budgets and identified through interviews with the site directors included funds received through other national or state programs and the implicit value of volunteer time. Some sites, for example, are eligible to apply for U.S. Department of Agriculture (USDA) meal reimbursements, and other sites are eligible to apply for federal E-rate funds to support technology, networking, and computer-related requirements. Some sites also reported significant volunteer time to assist with various program-related activities. Military personnel, for example, frequently volunteer in programs situated on military installations; other sites benefit from volunteers from local educational institutions and other members of the community. We asked site directors to estimate the number of volunteers, the number of hours per day, number of days per week, and number of weeks per cycle that volunteer services were provided. This information, together with an estimated wage rate for volunteers, was combined to estimate the implicit value of this volunteer time.[3]

Finally, we added a proportion of the costs incurred by NGB for administering the ChalleNGe program at the national level and providing oversight and support functions.[4] These costs include funding the training of ChalleNGe program staff (including travel and other related training expenses) and funding for an annual evaluation of program operations at each site. Total NGB administrative costs were allocated across the evaluation sites and class cycles in proportion to their share of the total number of admittees across all sites and class cycles in the relevant years.

---

[2] We excluded from these averages one site—Michigan—which reported a price per square foot of $7.58. The price per square foot for the remaining five sites ranged between $1.98 and $3.30.

[3] We assumed that volunteers with some college earn $13.97 per hour and those with a master's degree earn $26.03 per hour. These wages were estimated using data from the March 2010 CPS.

[4] NGB reported total costs of administering the ChalleNGe program of $7.2 million in 2005, $9.9 million in 2006, and $10.1 million in 2007.

Table 3.1 reports estimated operating costs averaged across the ten evaluation sites (so that each site contributes equally to the average) of $11,633 per admittee.[5] About 90 percent of these costs are accounted for in the site-level budgets. The remaining costs are largely accounted for by the implicit value of rent for those sites that did not account for that item in their budgets plus a share of NGB administrative costs. Other costs of operating the ChalleNGe program, such as the value of services rendered by other programs or by volunteers, while important for some sites, contribute little to the overall average cost per admittee.

Table 3.2 shows that there is considerable variation in site-level operating costs per admittee across the ten sites that participated in the ChalleNGe program evaluation. Variation in per admittee operating costs appears to be at least partly attributable to variation in program size. For example, total operating costs per admittee were $16,496 for the Fort McCoy, WI, site (which had 133 admittees during the evaluation) but only $6,758 for the Rantoul, IL, site (which had 1,490 admittees during the evaluation). Variation in wages and the price of other goods and services and in the nature of the programs themselves could account for variation in operating costs per admittee as well.

Table 3.1
Operating Cost per Admittee, by Source

Source of Cost	Operating Cost per Admittee ($2010)
Site-level costs	
Site-level budgets	10,416
Unaccounted facility rent/lease	345
USDA and E-rate funds	37
Volunteer time	18
Other[a]	38
Subtotal	10,854
NGB costs	779
Total costs	11,633

[a] Other operating costs include the receipt of Defense Reutilization and Marketing Office items, funds received through a 501 c(3) entity associated with the program, and other miscellaneous operating expenditures.

[5] Data obtained from the ChalleNGe Data and Management Reporting System indicated that a total of 4,741 applicants were admitted to the ChalleNGe program during these 18 class cycles. The difference between the total admitted during these class cycles and the 3,074 included in the program evaluation is accounted for by admittees who would have been under age 17 on the last day of the residential phase of the class cycle for which they applied and a small number of female admittees who were excluded from the evaluation (see Chapter Two).

Table 3.2
Site-Level Operating Costs per Admittee, by ChalleNGe Site

State	Site	Total Operating Cost ($2010)	No. of Admittees	Operating Cost per Admittee ($2010)
California	Camp San Luis Obispo	3,550,008	264	13,447
Florida	Camp Blanding	4,131,420	370	11,166
Georgia	Fort Gordon	4,415,080	460	9,598
Illinois	Rantoul	10,069,420	1,490	6,758
Michigan	Battle Creek	5,431,932	473	11,484
Mississippi	Camp Shelby	5,914,800	530	11,160
New Mexico	Roswell	1,684,071	153	11,007
North Carolina	Salemsburg	3,515,960	580	6,062
Texas	Galveston	3,272,832	288	11,364
Wisconsin	Fort McCoy	2,193,968	133	16,496

Opportunity Costs

Opportunity costs account for the value of time spent by individuals who participate in the ChalleNGe program but, unlike paid staff, are not directly compensated for their participation. We estimate these opportunity costs for three groups: applicants, cadets, and mentors/mentees (see Table 3.3). We also include in opportunity costs the value of some in-kind benefits received by cadets.

Applicants

An individual who wants to be admitted to the ChalleNGe program must spend time collecting information about the program, figuring out the procedures necessary to apply, and completing the requisite forms. To place a value on this time, we multiplied an estimate of the number of hours that an average applicant might spend in the application process by the average market wage for individuals without a high school diploma. We assumed that each applicant spent eight hours on the application process and valued those hours using the aver-

Table 3.3
Estimated Opportunity Cost of Time per Admittee, by Group

Group	Hours or Weeks	Wage ($2010)	Unit Cost ($2010)	PDV Cost per Admittee ($2010)
Applicants	8 hours	10.34/hour	83	110
Admittees	13.5 weeks	220/week	2,970	2,970
Mentors and mentees	40 hours	14.19/hour	568	292
All				3,372

NOTE: Estimates assume a social discount rate of 3 percent.

age wage of high school dropouts ($10.34 per hour as calculated from the March 2010 CPS). We then multiplied that product by the total number of applicants (3,074) participating in the ChalleNGe program evaluation and divided that quantity by the number of admittees (2,320) to arrive at an average cost per admittee of $110. We do not discount these costs, since we assume that they occurred within a few weeks or months of random assignment.

Cadets

A more significant source of opportunity costs is that incurred by cadets participating in the residential phase of the program. To place a value on this time, we use an estimate of the average weekly earnings of individuals in the ChalleNGe program evaluation control group that accounts for the fact that a significant percentage (29 percent) of individuals in the control group were not employed in the period between random assignment and the 9-month survey (Bloom, Gardenhire-Crooks, and Mandsager, 2009). We use the average annual earnings ($11,434) of the control group in the 12 months before the 36-month survey to estimate an average weekly wage of $220 (Millenky et al., 2011). The ChalleNGe program evaluation did not measure annual earnings at the time of the 9-month survey.

Cadets who graduate spend 22 weeks in the program. But only 53 percent of admittees graduate; 17 percent fail to enroll, another 15 percent do not complete the two-week pre-ChalleNGe residential phase, and another 15 percent do not complete the main 20-week residential phase (Bloom, Gardenhire-Crooks, and Mandsager, 2009). We assume that those who do not enroll spend no weeks in the program, those who do not complete the pre-ChalleNGe phase spend one week in the program, and those who do not complete the residential phase of the program spend 11 weeks in the program. These numbers imply, then, that on average, admittees spend 13.5 weeks in the program. Multiplying $220 by 13.5 weeks yields an opportunity cost of $2,970 per admittee.

Mentors and Mentees

In the post-residential phase of the ChalleNGe program, cadets are paired with individuals who mentor cadets over a one-year period. The work of mentors is voluntary, and neither the implicit value of their time nor the implicit value of the time spent by the cadet (the mentee) is included in the site budgets.[6] NGB (2008) reports that 99 percent of graduates are matched with a mentor at completion and, according to ChalleNGe guidelines, mentors must make contact with graduates at least once per week. However, both administrative data and the 9- and 21-month surveys suggest that compliance with this requirement is imperfect (Millenky, Bloom, and Dillon, 2010). We assume, on the basis of the 9-month survey, that 77 percent of graduates spend an average of one hour every two weeks with a mentor, for a combined (mentor plus mentee) expected total of 40 hours over the course of one year. We value those hours using the average wage of a high school graduate ($14.19 per hour as calculated from the March 2010 CPS). The assumption that both mentees and mentors have a high school diploma, on average, seems reasonable, since mentees will likely have slightly less education than this, on average, whereas mentors, on average, will likely have slightly more. These assumptions yield an opportunity cost per graduate of $568, or $301 per admittee. The

---

[6] Although mentors may receive utility from their volunteer activities, there is a real opportunity cost associated with spending their time on ChalleNGe rather than on some other volunteer or other productive activity.

present discounted value of this cost (the cost is incurred in the year following graduation) per admittee is $292.

In-Kind Benefits

Cadets benefit from a number of in-kind services while in residence, including meals, allowances, housing, and medical care. We account for the value of meals and allowances (an average of $1,314 per admittee) as negative opportunity costs, since these benefits effectively reduce the opportunity cost of participating in the program. The cost of meals would have been incurred by cadets and their parents had they not been admitted to the ChalleNGe program, and cadets benefit directly from the allowances. Other in-kind benefits provided during the residential phase of the program, such as housing and medical care, are not deducted from opportunity costs, since it is likely that the parents of cadets incur those costs regardless of program participation. It is unlikely that parents will drop their children from their health insurance or rent out their child's room while their child attends the ChalleNGe program, especially since high dropout rates imply that cadets, on average, spend considerably less than 22 weeks in residence.

Subtracting $1,314 from $3,372 (Table 3.3), yields net opportunity costs of $2,058 per admittee.

CHAPTER FOUR

Valuing Program Benefits

The principal benefit of the ChalleNGe program is to increase educational attainment, employment, and earnings of admittees (see Tables 2.3 and 2.4). Those treatment effects are observed at the time of the 36-month survey when the ChalleNGe admittees were, on average, only 20 years old. However, research suggests that the benefits of obtaining higher levels of education accrue over the entire lifetime. Thus, to estimate the full benefits of the ChalleNGe program, we must estimate how education affects lifetime earnings.[1] As discussed in Chapter Two, it is likely that higher educational attainment yields other nonpecuniary benefits over the life course as well (e.g., better health, less criminal activity, more civic engagement), but these relationships are less well-accepted and not as readily measured in available data. Consequently, our analysis focuses on lifetime earnings while recognizing that we likely underestimate the full benefit of higher educational attainment induced by the ChalleNGe program. We also value the effect of educational attainment on social welfare dependency and generate separate estimates of the value of the effect of ChalleNGe admission on criminal activity at the time of the 9- and 21-month surveys and on service to the community during the residential phase of the program.

This chapter presents our "baseline" benefit estimates assuming a social discount rate of 3 percent. We explore in Chapter Five the sensitivity of our baseline results to the assumed social discount rate and alternative methods to monetizing the value of educational attainment. These alternative approaches include using alternative specifications of the earnings regression, employing estimates of the causal effect of education on earnings obtained from the published literature, and using survey data for a more recent cohort of American youth.

Labor Market Earnings

Our approach to monetizing the value of higher educational attainment induced by the ChalleNGe program consists of two steps. In the first step, we estimate a model (by which we mean an empirically estimated statistical relationship) of lifetime earnings and educational attainment. In the second step, we use the parameter estimates from that model to impute the value of the estimated increase in educational attainment attributable to being admitted to the ChalleNGe program.

---

[1] Another approach would be to extrapolate from the earnings difference observed at the time of the 36-month survey. However, such an extrapolation would require us to make strong assumptions, with little or no support in available data, about the rate at which that earnings difference decays (or grows) over the life cycle.

We estimate a model of earnings and education using data from NLSY79, a nationally representative longitudinal survey of 12,686 men and women ages 14–22 in 1979.[2] With the exception of particular subsamples, these men and women were surveyed every year between 1979 and 1994 and biennially thereafter. By the time of the last available survey wave in 2008, the NLSY79 sample was between 43 and 51 years old. The longitudinal nature of the NLSY79 makes it particularly well-suited for our purposes, since, for a given individual, we can observe not only their educational attainment when they were age 20 but also their annual labor market earnings through their early 40s and beyond. The NLSY79 also has the advantage of including a measure of aptitude derived from the Armed Services Vocational Aptitude Battery (ASVAB) and measures of family background, which help isolate the effect of educational attainment on earnings from other confounding factors correlated with educational attainment.

We recognize that this type of regression is unlikely to fully account for the endogenous nature of educational attainment. We report alternative benefit estimates in Chapter Five derived from estimates of the causal effect of educational attainment on earnings reported in the published literature. These studies employ various "natural experiments" to untangle the effect of education from the effect of other confounding factors on earnings. However, we do not rely on those published causal estimates alone because it is not clear how well they generalize to the ChalleNGe program evaluation sample and the specific measures of educational attainment available in that evaluation.

We model earnings using the following regression specification:

$$PDVE_i = \alpha + \beta_1 GED_i + \beta_2 HS_i + \beta_3 SC_i + X_i \delta + \varepsilon_i \tag{1}$$

where $PDVE_i$ is the present discounted value of lifetime earnings of individual i; GED_i, HS_i, and SC_i are indicators for whether an individual earned a GED, earned a high school diploma, or attended some college by age 20; and X_i is a vector of covariates including age, gender, race/ethnicity (white, African-American, and Hispanic), Armed Forces Qualification Test (AFQT) percentile score (as derived from the ASVAB), parental education, and region of residence at age 20. ε_i is an idiosyncratic error term assumed to be uncorrelated with educational attainment and the variables in the vector X_i.

The vector of estimated coefficients $\hat{\beta}$ measures the correlation between educational attainment at age 20 and lifetime earnings. We measure educational attainment at age 20, since the ChalleNGe program evaluation results at 36 months, on average, are applicable to admittees of that age. The assumption of the model, then, is that education at age 20 is predictive of subsequent earnings, since individuals with higher levels of education at age 20, on average, will have higher levels of education at every subsequent age.

We construct $PDVE_i$ by summing discounted pretax labor market earnings reported at every available survey wave for a given individual plus 25 percent to account for the value of fringe benefits.[3] We impute earnings in the years in which the NLSY79 was not administered

---

[2] Our particular sample of 6,413 respondents excludes the military and poor-white subsamples and individuals with missing data on earnings and covariates. We also dropped respondents who were missing for more than five consecutive survey waves. To account for the potential undue influence of extreme earnings observations, we also drop the top 1 percent of earnings observations in each survey wave.

[3] Karoly (2008) reports that the range of fringe benefit rates used in cost-benefit analyses is from 13.7 to 37.6 percent. A rate of 25 percent is used in several analyses including Aos et al. (2004).

(every other year starting in 1995), in years in which particular survey respondents did not respond to the survey or the earnings question in particular, and between the last available survey wave and age 65 for each individual.[4] Age 65 is a typical stopping point for forecasting earnings effects in cost-benefit analyses, in part because labor force participation declines considerably after that point and in part because benefits that occur so far in the future contribute relatively little to total benefits because of discounting. Our imputations assume that earnings grow between missing survey waves at a real rate of 5.17 percent annually, which is the implied real annual rate of growth in earnings between ages 20 and 45 in our NLSY79 sample.

We assume that there is no real wage growth between the last observed age for any given individual in the NLSY79 and age 65. Empirical estimates of age-earnings profiles typically show a slight decline in real earnings between ages 50 and 65 attributable to a decline in hours of work (e.g., Murphy and Welch, 1990). This observation is based on current cohorts of older workers, however. The ChalleNGe cohorts will face a higher normal Social Security retirement age (age 67 rather than age 65) and, given budgetary pressures, lower pension, disability, and medical care benefits and perhaps even higher early and normal retirement ages than mandated under current law. These and other forces are likely to result in considerably higher labor force participation rates at older ages than observed in the past (Maestas and Zissimopoulos, 2010).

There is a close correspondence between the NLSY79 and ChalleNGe program evaluation measurements of GED and high school diploma receipt. However, the concept of "some college" is not measured equivalently in the two surveys. The ChalleNGe program evaluation 36-month survey asked: "Since [previous interview date], have you taken any college courses for credit? This would include courses at community, two-year, and four-year colleges." The 36-month survey did not ask whether respondents had finished their first year of college. Thus, we use a variable in the NLSY79 that indicates whether the respondent had attended at least 13 "grades" of school, where grade 13 is intended to be the first year of postsecondary education.

An issue with our measurement of "some college" is that it could be the case that individuals in the NLSY79 are more likely to have completed their first year of college than are individuals who took part in the ChalleNGe program evaluation, in which case the correlation between "some college" and earnings in the NLSY79 might overstate the correlation between "some college" and earnings in the ChalleNGe program evaluation. It is also possible that the NLSY79 population that attends some college is more likely to obtain four-year college and advanced degrees than is the ChalleNGe population that attends some college. To address this possibility, we present a range of estimates in Chapter Five that employ alternative specifications of the some college variable and restrict the NLSY79 sample to those who do not obtain four-year college or advanced degrees.

The same concern is relevant for vocational training, where it could be that the NLSY79 population claiming to have ever participated in vocational training is more likely to have completed vocational training than is the ChalleNGe program evaluation sample. As it turns out, though, vocational training has no independent effect on earnings in the NLSY79, and so this potential inconsistency is not of concern.

---

[4] An average of 2 percent of individuals in our NLSY79 sample have missing earnings data in any given survey year. The average age of the sample at the time of their last completed survey wave is 47.

We report the results of estimating Equation (1) in Table 4.1.[5] The results indicate large independent effects of having earned a high school diploma and attending some college on lifetime earnings. Having a high school diploma at age 20 increases PDVE by $137,210 relative to having no degree (GED or high school diploma), and having attended some college at age 20 increases PDVE by an additional $168,832. Both of these estimates are statistically significant at the 1 percent confidence level.

Our model implies that having earned a GED by age 20 has no statistically significant effect on lifetime earnings. The parameter estimate (–$23,439) is negative and imprecisely estimated. The effect of having participated in vocational training is positive ($39,364) but small in magnitude and statistically insignificant. These results are consistent with published studies on the effects of the GED and vocational training on earnings (e.g., Cameron and Heckman, 1993; Heckman and LaFontaine, 2006; Heckman, Lalonde, and Smith, 1999).[6] However, it is important to note that these results do not imply that the GED has no value whatsoever. It is possible that the GED has a positive effect on obtaining even higher levels of education, which in turn leads to higher earnings. But these indirect effects are accounted for in both Equation (1) and the ChalleNGe program evaluation (i.e., the educational categories as defined are not mutually exclusive).

Table 4.1
Estimated Effect of Educational Attainment at Age 20 on PDVE

Educational Attainment at Age 20	Estimated Effect of Educational Attainment on PDVE ($2010)
GED	–$23,439 [$51,300]
High school diploma	$137,201*** [$31,663]
Attended some college	$168,832*** [$25,805]
Vocational training	$39,364 [$28,766]
No. of observations	6,413
R-squared	0.279

DATA SOURCE: NLSY79.
NOTES: Regression also controls for age, gender, race/ethnicity, AFQT score, region of residence at age 20, and respondent's mother's and father's educational attainment. Estimates assume a social discount rate of 3 percent. The standard error of the estimate is reported in brackets.
***Statistically significant at the 1 percent confidence level.

---

[5]   We do not employ the NLSY79 survey weights, but, as we explain below, we do reweight regression results to account for gender and race/ethnicity differences between the NLSY79 and ChalleNGe program evaluation samples.

[6]   Clark and Jaeger (2006) report a positive effect of the GED, although only for certain subpopulations.

Table 4.2 shows how we use these parameter estimates to determine the value of the increase in educational attainment caused by being admitted to the ChalleNGe program. The second column of Table 4.2 records the weighted sum of parameter estimates obtained from estimating Equation (1) by gender and race/ethnicity, where the weights correspond to the proportion of the ChalleNGe program evaluation sample in each demographic group. This reweighting accounts for the fact that the ChalleNGe program evaluation sample contains a higher proportion of males, African-Americans, and Hispanics than does the NLSY79 sample (see Table 4.3). The table also makes explicit the fact that we assume that the effects of ChalleNGe on GED attainment and vocational training have no independent effect on lifetime earnings.

Table 4.2
Present Discounted Value of Increased Labor Market Earnings per Admittee

Benefit Source	Reweighted Estimated Effect of Educational Attainment on PDVE ($2010)	Estimated ChalleNGe Treatment Effect	PDV Benefit per Admittee ($2010)
Educational attainment at age 20			
GED	0	0.224	0
High school diploma	160,295	0.037	5,931
Attended some college	216,846	0.161	34,912
Vocational Training	0	0.070	0
Subtotal			40,843
Earnings at age 19 ($2010)		2,671	2,671
Total earnings benefit			43,514

NOTE: Estimates assume a social discount rate of 3 percent.

Table 4.3
Demographic Composition of the ChalleNGe Evaluation and NLSY79 Samples

Characteristic	ChalleNGe Evaluation Sample[a]	NLSY79 Sample
Male	0.876	0.480
Female	0.124	0.520
Hispanic	0.191	0.178
White	0.485	0.561
Black	0.324	0.261

[a] As reported in Millenky et al. (2011).

The third column of Table 4.2 reports the estimated treatment effect of being admitted to the ChalleNGe program on educational attainment at the time of the 36-month survey (as reported in Table 2.3). The estimated effect of the increase in educational attainment attributable to ChalleNGe admission on earnings per admittee is then the weighted sum of the figures reported in the second column, where the weights are given in the third column. The fourth column shows that the weighted sum of $40,843 is largely accounted for by the estimated effect of ChalleNGe admission on attending one or more years of college ($34,912). Although having a high school diploma has a substantial effect on lifetime earnings, the ChalleNGe program had relatively little effect on that outcome, and so the incremental effect of that outcome on ChalleNGe benefits is relatively small ($5,931).

Our baseline estimate of total earnings benefits per admittee ($43,514) includes the estimated effect of ChalleNGe on earnings in the year before the 36-month survey (i.e., at an average age of 19). We assume that ChalleNGe has no effect on earnings through educational attainment (or other pathways) at ages 17 or 18.

Cost of Education

It is standard in cost-benefit analyses to deduct the cost of obtaining higher levels of education from their associated benefits. We assume that the cost associated with the increase in GED attainment is included in the operating costs of the ChalleNGe program but that the cost of completing high school and obtaining a high school diploma and attending college is not. Using data from the NCES, and assuming that ChalleNGe admittees who obtain a high school diploma on average need to attend one more year of high school to achieve that diploma, we estimate that each additional high school diploma induced by the ChalleNGe program entails an additional $10,297 in costs.[7] Multiplying $10,297 by the estimated treatment effect for a high school diploma of 3.7 percent yields a cost of $381 per admittee, or $370 per admittee in present value terms under the assumption that those induced to finish high school do so, on average, one year after entering the study.[8]

According to NCES, total annual expenditures per full-time-equivalent student at public degree-granting colleges were $27,135 in the 2008–09 academic year.[9] This average is taken over both two- and four-year institutions, which is appropriate, since the "some college" outcome does not distinguish between the two types of institutions. In our NLSY79 sample, individuals who had attempted some college by age 20 completed an average of 1.13 years of college by age 30. Multiplying the average cost of attending one year of college, $27,135, by 1.13 years and then by 16 percent (the estimated effect of ChalleNGe admission on college attendance at the time of the 36-month survey) yields an average cost per admittee of college attendance of $4,906. Assuming that these additional years of college are accrued, on average,

---

[7] Digest of Educational Statistics (2010), Table 190.

[8] These calculations assume that only those admittees who are induced to obtain a high school diploma incur these costs. This assumption likely does not hold, since some admittees will attend high school but fail to obtain a diploma. For this reason, we likely underestimate total education costs induced by the program.

[9] Digest of Educational Statistics (2010).

at age 20, the present discounted value of these educational costs is $4,490 per admittee. Total education costs induced by the ChalleNGe program amount to $370 (high school) + $4,490 (college) = $4,860.

Social Welfare Dependency

Cost-benefit analyses of social programs typically account for the effect of the program on social welfare dependency, by which we mean receipt of cash transfers from income support programs. Social welfare dependency was not directly measured in the ChalleNGe program evaluation, and so we estimate this potential benefit by estimating the effect of educational attainment at age 20 on subsequent social welfare dependency using the approach just described, but where the dependent variable $PDVE_i$ in Equation (1) is replaced with the present discounted value of cash transfers received from federal and state welfare programs, Supplemental Security Income, and unemployment insurance.[10]

The results reported in Table 4.4 indicate that individuals who obtain a high school diploma and attend some college are less likely than high school dropouts to receive cash transfers. However, because the baseline probability of receiving cash transfers in any given year is low, the effect of educational attainment on the present discounted value of cash transfers is

Table 4.4
Estimated Effect of Educational Attainment at Age 20 on the PDV of Cash Transfers

Educational Attainment at Age 20	Estimated Effect of Educational Attainment on PDV of Cash Transfers ($2010)
GED	−$1,098 [$825]
High school diploma	−$6,268*** [$527]
Attended some college	−$1,888*** [$458]
Vocational training	−$439 [$429]
No. of observations	5,342
R-squared	0.12

DATA SOURCE: NLSY79.
NOTES: Regression also controls for age, gender, race/ethnicity, AFQT score, region of residence at age 20, and respondent's mother's and father's educational attainment. Estimates assume a social discount rate of 3 percent. The standard error of the estimate is reported in brackets.
***Statistically significant at the 1 percent confidence level.

---

[10] When missing, the value of cash transfers is imputed in the same manner as described for labor market earnings above.

relatively small—$6,268 for high school diploma recipients and an additional $1,888 for those attending one or more years of college by age 20. As with labor market earnings, our model implies that neither GED receipt nor vocational training has a statistically significant effect on the receipt of cash transfers.

Table 4.5 has the same structure as Table 4.2 showing the NLSY79 parameter estimates reweighted to account for the demographic composition of the ChalleNGe sample in the second column, the estimated treatment effects from the ChalleNGe program evaluation in the third column, and the estimated present discounted value of reduced social welfare expenditures per admittee in the fourth column, which totals $858 per admittee.

Since cash transfers are at once a cost for government and a benefit for recipients, the net effect of reduced cash transfers on the social benefits of the ChalleNGe program are zero, absent administrative costs. However, we assume that for every dollar transferred via these programs, 29 cents is spent on administrative costs. This estimate of administrative costs has been used in other cost-benefit analyses (e.g., Belfield et al., 2006; Heckman et al., 2010) and comes from an analysis of the proportion of funds transferred to the total costs of cash transfer programs. Thus, the net benefit per admittee of reducing social welfare dependency is 29 percent of $858, or $249.

Criminal Activity

The ChalleNGe program evaluation did not find statistically significant effects of ChalleNGe admission on criminal activity at the time of the 36-month survey. As a result, we do not value any long-term crime reduction benefits. However, the ChalleNGe program evaluation did find significant effects on criminal activity at the time of the 9- and 21-month surveys. This section describes how we value the short-run benefit of that reduction in criminal activity.

Table 4.5
Present Discounted Value of Reduced Social Welfare Dependency per Admittee

Benefit Source	Reweighted Estimated Effect of Educational Attainment on PDV of Cash Transfers ($2010)	Estimated ChalleNGe Treatment Effect	PDV Benefit per Admittee ($2010)
Educational attainment at age 20			
GED	0	0.224	0
High school diploma	−8,133	0.037	301
Attended some college	−3,462	0.161	557
Vocational Training	0	0.070	0
Subtotal			858
29% administrative cost			249

NOTE: Estimates assume a social discount rate of 3 percent.

The reduction in criminal activity attributable to the ChalleNGe program yields two types of benefits: (1) It reduces criminal justice costs and (2) it reduces costs incurred by the victims of crime. Table 4.6 lists the assumptions we make to value these benefits.

We use estimates reported in Karoly et al. (1998) to value reduced criminal justice costs. They assume that each arrest increases policing costs by $879 and adjudication costs by $1,832. Additionally, each day an individual spends in jail costs the government $38. The ChalleNGe program evaluation does not measure days in jail, so we assume, following Karoly et al. (1998), that individuals who are incarcerated spend an average of 16.6 days in jail. Finally, following Karoly et al. (1998), we assume that victim costs amount to 105 percent of criminal justice costs.[11]

The ChalleNGe program evaluation found that ChalleNGe admission reduced arrests at the time of the 9-month survey by 5.8 percentage points and incarceration by 8.2 percentage points. After reviewing responses to the 21-month survey, we assumed that each individual who was arrested at least once was arrested on average 1.37 times, and that each person incar-

Table 4.6
Present Discounted Value of Reduced Criminal Activity per Admittee

	Survey Wave		
	9 Month	21 Month	Both
Criminal justice costs per arrest[a]	$2,771	$2,771	
Victim costs per arrest[a]	$2,910	$2,910	
Treatment effect on arrests	−0.058	0.010	
Number of arrests per arrested[b]	1.370	1.370	
Reduction in arrests	0.079	−0.014	0.066
Arrest benefits per admittee	$451	−$78	$374
Costs per jail day[a]	38	38	
Victim cost per jail day[a]	40	40	
Treatment effect on incarceration	0.082	0.082	
Number of incarcerations per incarcerated[b]	1.370	1.370	
Days in jail per incarcerated[c]	22.742	22.742	
Reduction in jail days	1.865	1.865	3.730
Incarceration benefits per admitee	$145	$145	$291
Total	$597	$67	$664
PDV total	$597	$65	$662

NOTES: Estimates assume a social discount rate of 3 percent. All costs and benefits are reported in 2010 dollars.
[a] As reported in Karoly et al. (1998).
[b] As derived from Millenky, Bloom, and Dillon (2010).
[c] As derived from Karoly et al. (1998) and Millenky, Bloom, and Dillon (2010).

---

[11] Victim costs include the cost of all crimes that lead to a particular arrest.

cerated at least once was incarcerated 1.37 times.[12] Multiplying 1.37 by the estimated treatment effects yields a reduction in arrests of 0.08 per admittee and a reduction in jail days of 1.86 attributable to the ChalleNGe program. Multiplying these figures by the assumed criminal justice and victim cost figures cited in the previous paragraph yields a total benefit of $597 per admittee. Similar computations employing treatment effects estimated at the time of the 21-month survey show a benefit of −$78 for arrests (the parameter estimate for arrests is 0.01 at the time of the 21-month survey) and $145 for incarceration. Overall, then, we estimate that ChalleNGe admission yields a total present discounted value of $662 per admittee attributable to reduced criminal activity in the first two years following admission.

Service to the Community

One core component of the ChalleNGe program is service to the community. Examples of such service include tutoring in schools and after-school programs, charity fund raisers, visiting the elderly, roadway cleanup, sporting events, disaster preparedness, color guard, parades and fairs, and alcohol and drug awareness events in schools (Bloom, Gardenhire-Crooks, and Mandsager, 2009). The ChalleNGe program evaluation did not measure hours of service to the community, but NGB (2009) reports that cadets spend an average of 66 hours in service to the community activities during the residential phase of the program.[13]

We assume that these community services would not have been performed in the absence of ChalleNGe and that they can be valued using the average wage rate of a high school dropout ($10.34 per hour as calculated from the March 2010 CPS). Moreover, we assume that applicants not admitted to the ChalleNGe program perform none of these services during this 9-month period. Multiplying 66 hours by $10.34 per hour yields a benefit of service to the community of $682 per registered admittee (i.e., admittee completing the pre-ChalleNGe phase), or $423 per admittee.

---

[12] Millenky, Bloom, and Dillon (2010) show the proportions who have been arrested once and those who have been arrested more than once. Assuming that those in the latter category have been arrested exactly twice, this yields an average of 1.37 arrests among those who have been arrested at least once.

[13] We assume that this average is a weighted average across admittees who do and do not graduate from the program.

CHAPTER FIVE

Comparison of Costs and Benefits

This chapter begins with a comparison of the costs and benefits of the ChalleNGe program under the assumptions of the baseline model described in Chapters Three and Four and a presentation of how estimated costs and benefits are allocated across program stakeholders. We then show the sensitivity of the baseline estimates to variation in the social discount rate and deadweight loss factor and to alternative approaches to modeling the lifetime earnings effect of the ChalleNGe program.

Summary of Baseline Cost-Benefit Estimates

Table 5.1 summarizes our estimates of the costs and benefits of the ChalleNGe program under the baseline modeling assumptions. Assuming a deadweight loss factor of 15 percent, the present discounted value of operating and opportunity costs total $15,436, whereas the present discounted value of social benefits total $40,985.[1] Increased earnings attributable to the effect of ChalleNGe on educational attainment account for 94 percent of total benefits (net of the costs of college attendance).

Subtracting the estimated present discounted value of costs from benefits, we find that, for each admitted cadet, the program generates net benefits of $25,549. Total benefits are 2.66 times total costs, implying that the ChalleNGe program generates $2.66 in benefits for every dollar spent on the program. The estimated return on investment (net benefits divided by costs) in the ChalleNGe program is 166 percent. Because higher educational attainment yields benefits to individuals and society that are not fully captured in the outcomes considered here, it is likely that, all else equal, these benefit estimates understate the social return on investment in the ChalleNGe program, although to what extent is not known.

Allocation of Baseline Costs and Benefits Across Stakeholders

The baseline cost-benefit analysis implies that the ChalleNGe program generates a net positive return to society. As Table 5.2 shows, however, the costs and benefits of the ChalleNGe program accrue to different segments of society: government, program participants (admitted applicants), and program nonparticipants. For example, the operating costs of the program

---

[1] As explained in Chapter Two, the deadweight loss calculation applies to the change in tax revenue induced by the ChalleNGe program. On the benefit side, the specific formula applied is $0.15 \times 0.2 \times$ lifetime earnings $+ 2/3 \times 0.15 \times$ cost of education $+ 0.15 \times (1/0.29) \times$ social welfare dependency $+ 0.15 \times (1/2.05) \times$ criminal activity.

Table 5.1
Baseline Cost-Benefit Comparison

Item	PDV Benefit per Admittee ($2010)
Costs	
Operating costs	–$11,633
Opportunity costs	–$2,058
Deadweight loss of taxation (15%)	–$1,745
Total costs	–$15,436
Benefits	
Lifetime earnings	$43,514
Cost of education	–$4,860
Social welfare dependency	$249
Criminal activity	$662
Service to the community	$423
Deadweight loss of taxation (15%)	$997
Total benefits	$40,985
Cost-benefit comparison	
Net benefits	$25,549
Benefit-cost ratio	2.66
Return on investment	166%
Internal rate of return	6.4%

NOTE: Estimates assume a social discount rate of 3 percent.

are borne by the government, whereas the opportunity costs are largely borne by program participants. Increased earnings largely accrue to program participants, although a portion of those increased earnings accrue to the government in the form of increased tax revenue.[2] The government saves $859 in cash transfers, but program participants forgo that same amount. The government also saves $249 in administrative costs. The benefit of crime reduction is split roughly evenly between government and program nonparticipants. As might be expected, this allocation implies negative net benefits to government and large positive net benefits to program participants.

Sensitivity to Alternative Social Discount Rates and Deadweight Loss Factors

This section shows the sensitivity of the baseline cost-benefit comparisons to alternative assumptions about the social discount rate and deadweight loss of taxation.

---

[2]   Consistent with Karoly (2008) and Aos et al. (2004), we assume an average (federal, state, and local) income tax rate of 20 percent for this purpose. Also, see estimates of average federal tax rates published by the Congressional Budget Office.

Table 5.2
Allocation of Baseline Costs and Benefits per Admittee Across Stakeholders

Item	PDV Benefit ($2010)			
	Government	Program Participants	Program Nonparticipants	Total
Costs				
Operating costs (net of in-kind benefits)	–$10,319	$0	$0	–$10,319
In-kind benefits	–$1,314	$1,314	$0	$0
Opportunity costs	$0	–$3,080	–$292	–$3,372
Deadweight Loss (15%)	$0	$0	–$1,745	–$1,745
Total costs	–$11,633	–$1,766	–$2,037	–$15,436
Benefits				
Lifetime earnings	$8,703	$34,811		$43,514
Cost of education	–$3,240	–$1,620		–$4,860
Social welfare dependency	$1,107	–$858		$249
Criminal activity	$323		$339	$662
Service to the community			$423	$423
Deadweight Loss (15%)			$997	$997
Total benefits	$6,893	$32,333	$1,759	$40,985
Cost-benefit comparison				
Net benefits	–$4,740	$30,567	–$278	$25,549
Benefit-cost ratio	0.59	18.31	0.86	2.66

NOTE: Estimates assume a social discount rate of 3 percent.

Social Discount Rate

Figure 5.1 shows how estimated costs and benefits vary with social discount rates ranging between 1 and 8 percent. As can be seen in the figure, costs vary little with the social discount rate, since ChalleNGe costs occur largely in the present. However, benefits of ChalleNGe admission decline steeply with the social discount rate, since these benefits accrue over the full lifetime. As the figure shows, the present discounted value of benefits equals or exceeds costs when the social discount rate is at or below 6.4 percent (the internal rate of return) and falls below costs when the social discount rate is above 6.4 percent. The benefit-cost ratio is 2.66, 1.46, and 0.82 at social discount rates of 3, 5, and 7 percent.

Deadweight Loss Factor

Figure 5.2 shows how the estimated benefit-cost ratio varies with deadweight loss factors ranging between 0 and 100 percent of the change in tax revenue induced by the ChalleNGe program (i.e., the costs and benefits listed in the government column of Table 5.2) for social discount rates of 3 and 5 percent. At a social discount rate of 3 percent, the benefit-cost ratio

Figure 5.1
ChalleNGe Costs and Benefits per Admittee as a Function of the Social Discount Rate

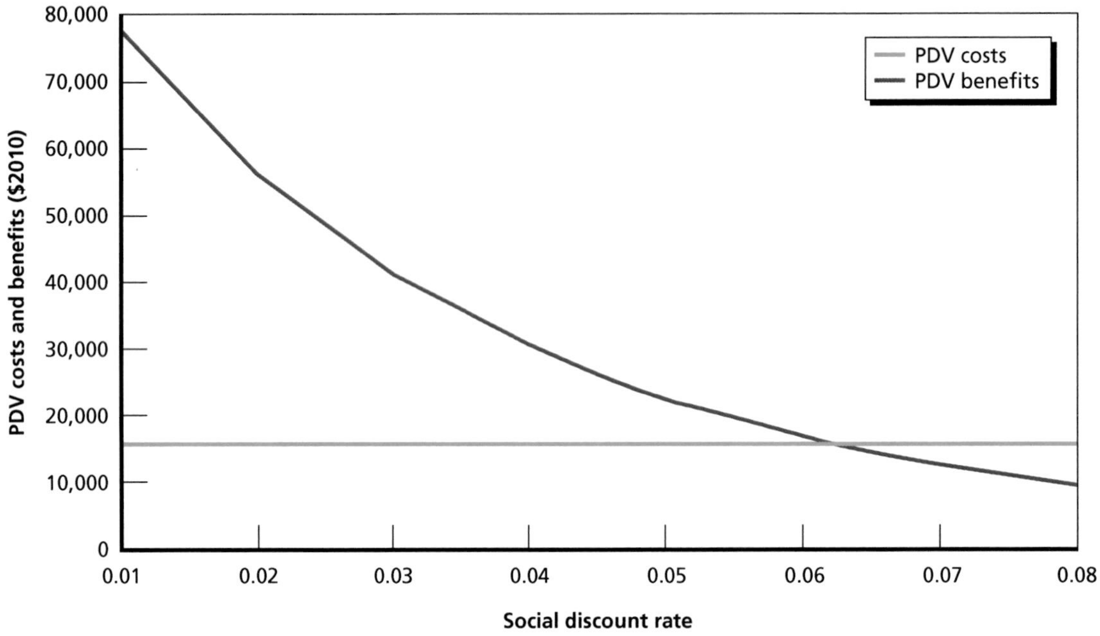

NOTE: Estimates assume a social discount rate of 3 percent and a deadweight loss factor of 15 percent.
RAND *TR1193-5.1*

is considerably above 1 for any deadweight loss factor between 0 and 100 percent. At a social discount rate of 5 percent, the estimated benefit-cost ratio falls below 1 for deadweight loss factors above 99 percent.

Alternative Models of Lifetime Earnings Effects

Tables 5.3 and 5.4 present estimated net benefits and benefit-cost ratios in which we compute estimated earnings benefits employing six different models, for three different social discount rates, and assuming a deadweight loss factor of 15 percent. The six different earnings models (explained in detail in the appendix) are as follows:

- **Baseline model**.
- **Complete less than one year of college model**. This model assumes that the effect of ChalleNGe admission is to increase the probability of attending one year of college by age 20 but not the probability of completing that year of college.
- **No postsecondary degree models**. These two models assume that the effect of ChalleNGe admission is to increase the probability of attending one year of college by age 20 but not to increase the probability of (1) obtaining an advanced or professional degree such as a master's or law degree or (2) more restrictively, a four-year college degree.
- **NLSY97 model**. This model employs data from the NLSY97, a nationally representative cohort of American youth ages 12–18 in 1997. This model has the advantage of estimating the effect of education on earnings in a birth cohort that is closer in age to the

Figure 5.2
ChalleNGe Cost-Benefit Ratio as a Function of Deadweight Loss Factor and the Social Discount Rate

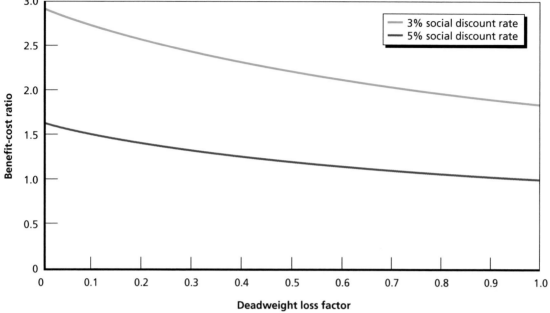

Table 5.3
Net Benefit per Admittee, by Lifetime Earnings Model and Social Discount Rate

Earnings Model	Social Discount Rate ($2010)		
	3%	5%	7%
Baseline	25,596	7,096	–2,711
Complete less than one year of college	12,032	1,692	–4,080
No advanced or professional degree	21,905	4,936	–4,165
No four-year college degree	8,330	–2,314	–8,176
NLSY97	33,474	15,889	5,862
Causal effect of education	26,378–61,395	9,564–32,857	771–16,660

NOTE: Estimates assume a deadweight loss factor of 15 percent.

ChalleNGe program evaluation sample but has the disadvantage of observing their labor market earnings only through ages 24–29 (the last available survey wave is 2009).

- **Causal effect of education model.** Estimating the effect of education on earnings is complicated by the fact that we cannot observe all of the factors that affect both educational attainment and earnings. This model employs parameter estimates reported in published studies that employ "natural experiments" to isolate the causal effect of education on earnings.

Table 5.4
Benefit-Cost Ratio, by Lifetime Earnings Model and Social Discount Rate

Earnings Model	Social Discount Rate		
	3%	5%	7%
Baseline	2.66	1.46	0.82
Complete less than one year of college	1.78	1.11	0.74
No advanced or professional degree	2.42	1.32	0.73
No four-year college degree	1.54	0.85	0.47
NLSY97	3.17	2.03	1.38
Causal effect of education	2.71–4.98	1.62–3.13	1.05–2.08

NOTE: Estimates assume a deadweight loss factor of 15 percent.

The tables show that estimated net benefits and benefit-cost ratios are sensitive to lifetime-earnings modeling assumptions and the choice of the social discount rate. The "complete less than one year of college" and "no four-year degree" models yield the lowest benefit-cost ratios, which is not surprising, since the estimated effect of college attendance is significantly attenuated if we assume that ChalleNGe admission has no effect on college completion by age 20 or, alternatively, on eventual completion of a four-year college degree. At a social discount rate of 3 percent, these models yield benefit-cost ratios above 1 (1.78 and 1.54, respectively), but at social discount rates of 5 and 7 percent, the benefit-cost ratio is close to or below 1. Assuming, less restrictively, that ChalleNGe admission has no effect on the probability of obtaining an advanced or professional degree results in a slight reduction in the benefit-cost ratio to 2.42.

The NLSY97 model, on the other hand, results in a higher benefit-cost ratio, because that model shows a substantial positive effect of GED completion on labor market earnings received in one's twenties. This is an intriguing result, since the consensus of researchers using the NLSY79 is that the GED has no effect on labor market earnings (Cameron and Heckman, 1993; Heckman and LaFontaine, 2006). As we note above, however, we are reluctant to emphasize these results because the NLSY97 cohort is still relatively young, and so we must project earnings effects far into the future and because we are not aware of any published work on GED receipt and earnings in this more recent cohort; more work needs to be done to corroborate this finding of an apparent increase in the return to GED attainment over time.

The "causal effect of education" model also yields higher estimates of the benefit-cost ratio than does the baseline model, but these models require that we make assumptions about the persistence of the employment effects estimated at the time of the 36-month survey. We assume that the estimated employment effect at 36 months (7.1 percent) persists for between 10 and 45 years. The greater is the assumed persistence of the employment effects, the higher is the estimated benefit-cost ratio.

CHAPTER SIX

Conclusions

The best available evidence indicates that admission to the ChalleNGe program has substantial positive effects on educational attainment. The analyses described in this report suggest that the social benefits of this increase in educational attainment in terms of higher lifetime labor market earnings (as well as smaller benefits associated with a decrease in criminal activity and social welfare dependency and an increase in service to the community) outweigh the social costs of operating the ChalleNGe program. Under our baseline modeling assumptions, benefits outweigh costs by a factor of 2.66 to 1, implying that the program yields $2.66 in benefits for every dollar in costs.

However, it is important to acknowledge that this "baseline" benefit-cost ratio is sensitive to the approach taken to forecasting future earnings of ChalleNGe admittees, the social discount rate, and the deadweight loss factor. At a social discount rate of 3 percent and deadweight loss factor of 15 percent, the most conservative estimate of the benefit-cost ratio is 1.54, which assumes that ChalleNGe admission has no effect on the probability of obtaining a four-year college degree. On the other hand, employing widely cited returns to educational attainment published in the economics literature or data from the more recent NLSY97 yields benefit-cost ratios of 2.71–4.98 and 3.17, respectively.

Because the earnings benefits attributable to higher education occur in the future, whereas the costs of the ChalleNGe program occur in the present, the benefit-cost ratio declines rapidly with the social discount rate. At social discount rates above 6.4 percent, the ChalleNGe program no longer yields positive social returns under the assumptions of our baseline model. The benefit-cost ratio, though, is not nearly as sensitive to the choice of deadweight loss factor, since deadweight loss increases both costs and benefits.

Under baseline assumptions, these cost-benefit comparisons suggest that continued operation of existing ChalleNGe sites will yield substantial net benefits, albeit largely in the form of private benefits to program participants from higher earnings rather than benefits to the public sector and other members of society. This analytical conclusion supports continued investment in the ChalleNGe program, especially considering that educational attainment likely yields benefits to individuals and society that are not fully captured in the outcomes considered here and that the estimated return on investment in the ChalleNGe program is considerably higher than that estimated for other rigorously evaluated social programs that seek to alter the life-course of disadvantaged youth and young adults.

For example, Job Corps, a full-time residential program providing education, vocational training, and job placement services for at-risk youth who have dropped out of school, is arguably the closest model to the ChalleNGe program. A random assignment evaluation of the program showed positive effects on GED completion and vocational training certification but not on high school diploma receipt or college attendance (Schochet, McConnell, and Burghardt, 2003). The positive effect of the program on labor market earnings estimated 3–4 years after random assignment were not evident in years 5–7. Favorable effects of Job Corps admission on crime were also found four years following random assignment. Nevertheless, a cost-benefit analysis by Schochet, McConnell, and Burghardt (2003) found that costs exceeded benefits for the full evaluation sample, although there was some evidence suggesting a modest return on investment in Job Corps for the older youth ages 20–24. Other examples include Big Brothers Big Sisters, a program that provides one-on-one mentoring for at-risk youth, and state-run welfare-to-work programs. Aos et al. (2004) estimates a benefit-cost ratio of 1.01 for Big Brothers Big Sisters, whereas Greenberg, Deitch, and Hamilton (2010) reports that net benefits to society for 28 welfare-to-work programs (as measured in random assignment evaluations) never exceed $2,000 per participant.

The extent to which the cost-benefit estimates reported here lend support to proposals to expand the ChalleNGe program to serve more youth depends on several additional factors. First, program effects achieved at the ChalleNGe evaluation sites must be generalizable to future applicant cohorts. This is perhaps reasonable to assume provided that the program continues to serve what appears to be a relatively advantaged population of high school dropouts. Second, one must assume that the average cost of serving a larger population of dropouts does not increase significantly relative to the estimated benefits. Again, this may be reasonable to assume provided that the program expansion targets a similar-situated population of dropouts.

Alternative Models of Lifetime Earnings Effects

This appendix describes the five alternative models of lifetime earnings effects listed in Chapter Five and Table 5.3. All benefit estimates assume a social discount rate of 3 percent.

Complete Less Than One Year of College Model

As explained in Chapter Four, an issue with our measurement of "some college" is that it could be the case that individuals in the NLSY79 are more likely to have completed their first year of college than individuals in the ChalleNGe program evaluation, in which case the correlation between "some college" and earnings in the NLSY79 might overstate the correlation between "some college" and earnings in the ChalleNGe program evaluation. The alternative model we describe here makes the strong assumption that ChalleNGe admission increases the probability of attending one year of college by age 20 but has virtually no effect on the probability of completing that year of college.

We operationalize this assumption by adding variables to Equation (1) that measure whether the respondent had completed one or more years of college by age 20 or had received an associate's degree or more. As can be seen in Table A.1, the effect of adding these variables to the model is to significantly reduce the marginal effect of attending college from $216,846 (Table 4.2) to $80,378. Making the conservative assumption that ChalleNGe admission increases the probability of completing one or more years of college by age 20 by only 0.8 percent (the estimated treatment effect of receiving any college degree—see Table 2.3) reduces the estimated lifetime earnings effect of ChalleNGe admission from $43,514 (Table 4.2) to $25,202.

No Postsecondary Degree Models

One might also worry that the NLSY79 population that completes a year of college by age 20 is more likely to eventually obtain a college or advanced degree than is the ChalleNGe population. Individuals who drop out of high school, even those qualified and motivated to participate in ChalleNGe, have perhaps demonstrated a weaker commitment to schooling than the overall population, and so even if they complete some college, they may be less likely to eventually complete a college degree. To examine the sensitivity of our earnings benefits estimates to this assumption, we estimated Equation (1) limiting the sample to individuals who never complete an advanced or professional degree (e.g., master's degree, law degree, medical

Table A.1
Lifetime Earnings Benefit per Admittee Assuming Limited College Completion

Benefit Source	Reweighted Estimated Effect of Educational Attainment on PDVE ($2010)	Estimated ChalleNGe Treatment Effect (36-Month Survey)	PDV Benefit per Admittee ($2010)
Educational attainment at age 20			
GED	0	0.224	0
High school diploma	179,009	0.037	6,623
Attended some college	80,378	0.161	12,941
Completed some college	256,914	0.008	2,055
Associate's degree	113,894	0.008	911
Vocational training	0	0.070	0
Subtotal			22,531
Earnings at age 19 ($2010)		2,671	2,671
Total earnings benefits			25,202

NOTE: Estimates assume a social discount rate of 3 percent.

degree, Ph.D.) and then, even more restrictively, to individuals who never complete a four-year college degree. Restricting the sample to individuals who never complete an advanced or professional degree reduces the estimated earnings benefits to $40,401 (Table A.2), and restricting the sample to individuals who never complete a four-year college degree reduces the estimated earnings benefits to $27,313 (Table A.3).

NLSY97 Model

The weakness of using the NLSY79 to model earnings and education is that those results apply to a cohort that is considerably older than the cohort participating in the ChalleNGe program evaluation. If the returns to education are changing over time (see, for example, Card and DiNardo, 2002), then we risk over- or underestimating lifetime earnings effects by relying on an older cohort. An alternative data set is the NLSY97, which has a similar structure to the NLSY79 but surveys a cohort that is closer in age to the ChalleNGe program evaluation sample (although still considerably older on average, ages 21–27 in 2006). The drawback of using the NLSY97 is that we can observe their earnings only through ages 24–30.

Table A.4 shows the result of estimating Equation (1) for both the NLSY79 and NLSY97 cohorts restricting the sample to individuals ages 26–29.[1] The most striking difference between the two cohorts is the emergence of a positive and significant effect of GED attainment and vocational training in the NLSY97 sample. To our knowledge, this finding has not been

---

[1] We extrapolate earnings through age 65 in both the NLSY79 and NLSY97 samples, employing observed earnings growth rates in our main NLSY79 sample through age 45 and assuming no real earnings growth thereafter.

Table A.2
Lifetime Earnings Benefit per Admittee Assuming No Advanced or Professional Degree

Benefit Source	Reweighted Estimated Effect of Educational Attainment on PDVE ($2010)	Estimated ChalleNGe Treatment Effect	PDV Benefit per Admittee ($2010)
Educational attainment at age 20			
GED	0	0.224	0
High school diploma	153,253	0.037	5,670
Attended some college	199,125	0.161	32,059
Vocational training	0	0.07	0
Subtotal			37,730
Earnings at age 19 ($2010)		2,671	2,671
Total earnings benefit			40,401

NOTE: Estimates assume a social discount rate of 3 percent.

Table A.3
Lifetime Earnings Benefit per Admittee Assuming No Four-Year College Degree

Benefit Source	Reweighted Estimated Effect of Educational Attainment on PDVE ($2010)	Estimated ChalleNGe Treatment Effect	PDV Benefit per Admittee ($2010)
Educational attainment at age 20			
GED	0	0.224	0
High school diploma	144,902	0.037	5,361
Attended some college	119,754	0.161	19,280
Vocational training	0	0.07	0
Subtotal			24,642
Earnings at age 19 ($2010)		2,671	2,671
Total earnings benefit			27,313

NOTE: Estimates assume a social discount rate of 3 percent.

reported in the published literature and stands in stark contrast to widely cited estimates of the effect of the GED on labor market earnings based on the earlier NLSY79 cohort (Cameron and Heckman, 1993; Heckman and LaFontaine, 2006). The estimated effect of receiving a high school diploma and attending some college is similar across the two cohorts. Vocational training has positive and significant effects on PDVE in both cohorts, although of a considerably smaller magnitude than those observed for educational attainment.

Table A.4
Estimated Effect of Educational Attainment on PDVE Through Ages 26–29 in the NLSY79 and NLSY97

	Estimated Effect of Educational Attainment on PDVE ($2010)	
	NLSY79	NLSY97
Educational Attainment at Age 20		
GED	$7,360 [$36,166]	$116,932** [$47,184]
High school diploma	$184,906*** [$23,273]	$179,423*** [$34,225]
Attended some college	$115,987*** [$20,085]	$118,759*** [$26,001]
Vocational training	$50,402** [$22,669]	$63,185** [$29,258]
No. of observations	6,413	3,393
R-squared	0.24	0.12

DATA SOURCES: NLSY79 and NLSY97.
NOTES: Samples restricted to individuals ages 26–29. Regressions also control for age, gender, race/ethnicity, AFQT score, region of residence at age 20, and respondent's mother's and father's educational attainment. Estimates assume a discount rate of 3 percent. The standard error of the estimate is reported in brackets.
**Statistically significant at the 5 percent confidence level.
***Statistically significant at the 1 percent confidence level.

Extrapolating these earnings effects to age 65 yields lifetime earnings benefits of $33,424 per admittee using the NLSY79 and $59,046 per admittee using the NLSY97.[2]

Causal Effect of Education Model

The causal effect of education on wages has been widely studied in the labor economics literature. The approach described here consists of employing estimates reported in the published literature and applying them to the estimated treatment effects from the MDRC evaluation. We selected three widely cited estimates of the causal return to high school education and three estimates of the causal return to college education (see Table A.5).[3]

To apply these estimates, we first calculated PDVE for the average high school dropout in the NLSY79.[4] To estimate the return to a high school diploma, we multiplied that figure ($618,523) by the estimated return to an additional year of high school education (which ranges between 8 and 10 percent). We then multiplied those figures by the estimated treatment

[2] Note that the NLSY79 earnings benefit estimate in Table A.4 differs from that reported in Table 4.2 because the sample in Table A.4 is restricted to individuals ages 26–29.

[3] There are no studies that employ a "natural experiment" design to estimate the effect of a GED credential on earnings. However, two widely cited studies, Cameron and Heckman (1993) and Heckman and LaFontaine (2006) find little or no effect of the GED on earnings, controlling for ability and family background characteristics.

[4] Reweighted to reflect the demographic characteristics of the ChalleNGe sample.

Table A.5
Estimates of the Causal Effect of Educational Attainment on Hourly Wages

Educational Outcome/Source	Method	Estimated Effect on Hourly Wage, %
Heckman and LaFontaine (2006)	Ordinary least squares with rich set of controls	0
Ashenfelter and Rouse (1998)	Estimates from a sample of twins	9
Angrist and Krueger (1991)	Instrument with interaction of quarter of birth and compulsory schooling laws	8–10
Staiger and Stock (1997)	Instrument with quarter of birth (limited information maximum likelihood)	8–10
Kane and Rouse (1995)	Instrument with college proximity (returns to two-year college)	9
Card (1995)	Instrument with college proximity	9–13
Carneiro, Hechman, and Vytlacik (2011)	Instrument with college proximity and local unemployment	8–11

effect on receipt of a high school diploma (3.7 percent) to generate the effect of ChalleNGe admission on earnings attributable to high school diploma attainment. We employed the same method to estimate earnings effects attributable to college attendance. Summing those earnings effects across educational categories yields a total estimated earnings benefit of $13,671 when using the lowest estimates of the returns to schooling and $21,349 when using the highest estimates.

These estimates account for the increase in wages attributable to educational attainment but not for any increase in labor force participation. However, it is conceivable that educational attainment increases labor force participation too by reducing unemployment or increasing hours worked among those who work. In fact, the MDRC evaluation shows that ChalleNGe admission increases employment by 7.1 percentage points, although it is not known whether that employment effect is attributable to the program's education effects. If these employment effects persist at all future ages, the total effect of ChalleNGe admission on lifetime earnings in this model is $71,776 (using the low range of returns to schooling). If we assume that MDRC's estimated employment effect decays over ten years, the total effect of ChalleNGe admission on lifetime earnings in this model is then $44,357 (again, using the low range of returns to schooling).

Bibliography

Angrist, Joshua, and Alan Krueger. 1991. Does Compulsory School Attendance Affect Schooling and Earnings? *The Quarterly Journal of Economics* 106(4): 979–1014.

Aos, Steve, Roxanne Lieb, Jim Mayfield, Marna Miller, and Annie Pennucci. 2004. *Benefits and Costs of Prevention and Early Intervention Programs for Youth.* Olympia, Wash.: Washington Institute for Public Policy.

Ashenfelter, Orley, and Cecilia Rouse. 1998. Income, Schooling, and Ability: Evidence from a New Sample of Identical Twins. *The Quarterly Journal of Economics* 113(1): 253–284.

Ashenfelter, Orley, Colm Harmon, and Hessel Oosterbeek. 1999. A Review of Estimates of the Schooling/ Earnings Relationship, with Tests for Publication Bias. *Labour Economics* 6(4): 453–70.

Barnett, Steven W., Clive R. Belfield, and Milagros Nores. 2005. Lifetime Cost-Benefit Analysis, in Lawrence J. Schweinhart, Jeanne Montie, Zongping Xiang, Steven W., Barnett, Clive R. Belfield, and Milagros Nores (eds.). Lifetime Effects: The High/Scope Perry Preschool Study Through Age 40, *Monographs of the High/Scope Educational Research Foundation,* No. 14. Ypsilanti, Mich.: High/Scope Press.

Belfield, Clive R., Milagros Nores, Steve Barnett, and Lawrence Schweinhart. 2006. The High/Scope Perry Preschool Program: Cost-Benefit Analysis Using Data from the Age-40 Followup. *Journal of Human Resources* 41(1): 162–90.

Black, Sandra E., Paul J. Devereux, and Kjell G. Salvanes. 2008. Staying in the Classroom and Out of the Maternity Ward? The Effect of Compulsory Schooling Laws on Teenage Births. *The Economic Journal* 118: 1025–54.

Bloom, Dan, Alissa Gardenhire-Crooks, and Conrad Mandsager. 2009. *Reengaging High School Dropouts: Early Results of the National Guard Youth ChalleNGe Program Evaluation.* New York: MDRC.

Cameron, Stephen V., and James J. Heckman. 1993. The Nonequivalence of High School Equivalents. *Journal of Labor Economics* 11(1): 1–47.

Card, David. 1995. Using Geographic Variation in College Proximity to Estimate the Return to Schooling, in Louis E. Christofides, Kenneth Grant, and Robert Swindinsky (eds.). *Aspects of Labour Economics: Essays in Honor of John Vanderkamp.* Toronto: University of Toronto Press.

————. 1999. The Causal Effect of Education on Earnings in Orley Ashenfelter and David Card (eds.). *The Handbook of Labor Economics,* Volume 3. Amsterdam: Elsevier Science B.V.

Card, David, and John E. DiNardo. 2002. Skill-Biased Technological Change and Rising Wage Inequality: Some Problems and Puzzles. *Journal of Labor Economics* 20(4): 733–83.

Carneiro, Pedro, James J. Heckman, and Edward J. Vytlacil. 2011. Estimating Marginal Returns to Education. *American Economic Review* 101(6): 2754–81.

CBO—*See* Congressional Budget Office.

ChalleNGe, website, no date. As of November 8, 2011:
http://www.ngycp.org

Chapman, Chris, Jennifer Laird, Nicole Ifill, and Angelina KewalRamani. 2011. *Trends in High School Dropout and Completion Rates in the United States: 1972–2009.* Washington, D.C.: U.S. Department of Education, National Center for Education Statistics.

Clark, Melissa A., and David A. Jaeger. 2006. Natives, the Foreign-Born and High School Equivalents: New Evidence on the Returns to the GED. *Journal of Population Economics* 19: 769–93.

Congressional Budget Office, estimates of federal tax rates. As of January 14, 2012:
http://www.cbo.gov/publications/collections/collections.cfm?collect=13

Department of Defense, Department of Defense Instruction (DoDI) 1025.8, 2002.

Digest of Educational Statistics, 2010. As of January 14, 2012:
http://nces.ed.gov/programs/digest/d10/

GAO—*See* U.S. Government Accountability Office.

Greenberg, David H., Victoria Deitch, and Gayle Hamilton. 2010. A Synthesis of Random Assignment Benefit-Cost Studies of Welfare-to-Work Programs. *Journal of Benefit-Cost Analysis* 1(1): Article 3.

Heckman, James J., and Paul A. LaFontaine. 2006. Bias Corrected Estimates of GED Returns. *Journal of Labor Economics* 24(3): 661–700.

———. 2010. The American High School Graduation Rate: Trends and Levels. *Review of Economics and Statistics* 92(2): 244–62.

Heckman, James J., Robert J. Lalonde, and Jeffrey A. Smith. 1999. The Economics and Econometrics of Active Labor Market Programs, in Orley Ashenfelter and David Card (eds.). *Handbook of Labor Economics*, Volume 3. Amsterdam: Elsevier Science B.V.

Heckman, James J., Seong Hyeok Moon, Rodrigo Pinto, Peter A. Savelyev, and Adam Yavitz. 2010. The Rate of Return to the HighScope Perry Preschool Program. *Journal of Public Economics* 94: 114–28.

Kane, Thomas J., and Cecilia Elena Rouse. 1995. Labor-Market Returns to Two- and Four-Year College. *American Economic Review* 85(3): 600–614.

Karoly, Lynn A. 2008. *Valuing Benefits in Benefit-Cost Studies of Social Programs.* Santa Monica, Calif.: RAND Corporation. TR-643-MCF. As of January 26, 2012:
http://www.rand.org/pubs/technical_reports/TR643.html

Karoly, Lynn A., Peter W. Greenwood, Susan S. Everingham, Jill Hoube, M. Rebecca Kilburn, C. Peter Rydell, Matthew Sanders, and James Chiesa. 1998. *Investing in Our Children: What We Know and Don't Know About the Costs and Benefits of Early Childhood Interventions.* Santa Monica, Calif.: RAND Corporation. MR-898-TCWF. As of January 26, 2012:
http://www.rand.org/pubs/monograph_reports/MR898.html

Lochner, Lance. 2011. Non-Production Benefits of Education: Crime, Health, and Good Citizenship. NBER Working Paper #16722. Cambridge, Mass.: National Bureau of Economic Research.

Lochner, Lance, and Enrico Moretti. 2004. The Effect of Education on Crime: Evidence from Prison Inmates, Arrests, and Self-Reports. *American Economic Review* 59: 75–103.

Maestas, Nicole, and Julie Zissimopoulos. 2010. How Longer Work Lives Ease the Crunch of Population Aging. *Journal of Economic Perspectives* 24(1): 139–60.

McCaul, Edward J., Gordon A. Donaldson, Theodore Coladarci, and William E. Davis. 1992. Consequences of Dropping out of School: Findings from High School and Beyond. *Journal of Educational Research* 85(4): 198–207.

Millenky, Megan, Dan Bloom, and Colleen Dillon. 2010. *Making the Transition: Interim Results of the National Guard Youth ChalleNGe Evaluation.* New York: MDRC.

Millenky, Megan, Dan Bloom, Sara Muller-Ravett, and Joseph Broadus. 2011. *Staying on Course: Three-Year Results of the National Guard Youth ChalleNGe Evaluation.* New York: MDRC.

Moretti, Enrico. 2004. Estimating the Social Return to Higher Education: Evidence from Longitudinal and Repeated Cross-Sectional Data. *Journal of Econometrics* 121: 175–212.

Murphy, Kevin M., and Finis Welch. 1990. Empirical Age-Earnings Profiles. *Journal of Human Resources* 8(2): 202–29.

NGB—*See* National Guard Bureau.

National Guard Bureau. 2008. *National Guard Youth ChalleNGe Program: 2007 Performance and Accountability Highlights.* Washington, D.C.

———. 2009. *National Guard Youth ChalleNGe Program: 2010 Performance and Accountability Highlights.* Washington, D.C.

———. 2011. *National Guard Youth ChalleNGe Program: 2010 Performance and Accountability Highlights.* Washington, D.C.

Office of Management and Budget. 1992. *Guidelines and Discount Rates for Benefit-Cost Analysis of Federal Programs (Revised).* Circular No. A-94. Washington, D.C. As of January 26, 2012: http://www.whitehouse.gov/omb/circulars/a094/a094.html

OMB—*See* Office of Management and Budget.

Oreopoulos, Philip. 2007. Do Dropouts Drop Out Too Soon? Wealth, Health, and Happiness from Compulsory Schooling. *Journal of Public Economics* 91: 2213–29.

Oreopoulos, Philip, and Kjell G. Salvanes. 2011. Priceless: The Nonpecuniary Benefits of Schooling. *Journal of Economic Perspectives* 25(1): 159–84.

Schochet, Peter Z., Sheena McConnell, and John Burghardt. 2003. *National Job Corps Study: Findings Using Administrative Earnings Records Data.* Princeton, N.J.: Mathematica Policy Research.

Staiger, Douglas, and James Stock. 1997. Instrumental Variables Regressions with Weak Instruments. *Econometrica* 65(3): 557–86.

U.S. Government Accountability Office. 1991. *Discount Rate Policy.* Washington, D.C.